CONTENTS

A royal visit

Welcome to the Murderous Maths Organization!

You've picked a good time to join us because we're having a royal visit to celebrate our first 13 years of strange numbers, odd shapes, tricks, illusions and puzzles. We're going to take you on the first ever tour around the MM building. Along the way you'll get to see the Number Vaults, the Inside-out Room, the Research Lab, the Department of Random Thinking and loads more!

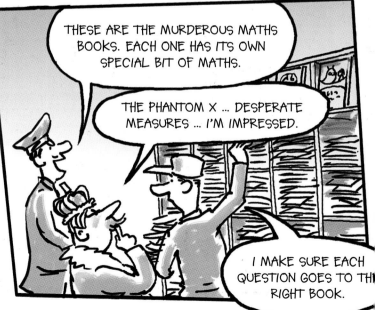

THE MURDEROUS MATHS OF EVERYTHING

KJARTAN POSKITT

illustrated by ROB DAVIS

For Bridget, Maisie, Florence, Dulcie and Miranda.

With thanks to Michael Jones, Rob Eastaway and Diana Kimpton for their help, ideas and checking the sums!

Scholastic Children's Books
Euston House
24 Eversholt Street
London
NW1 1DB

A division of Scholastic Ltd
London ~ New York ~ Toronto ~ Sydney ~ Auckland
Mexico City ~ New Delhi ~ Hong Kong

Editorial Director: Lisa Edwards
Editors: Victoria Garrard, Stefanie Smith and Catriona Clarke

First published in the UK by Scholastic Ltd, 2010
This edition published 2011

Text copyright © Kjartan Poskitt, 2010
Illustrations copyright © Rob Davis, 2010
Illustrations by Rob Davis based on an original artwork style created by Philip Reeve
All rights reserved

ISBN 978 1407 13143 6

Printed and bound by Tien Wah Press Pte. Ltd, Malaysia

2 4 6 8 10 9 7 5 3 1

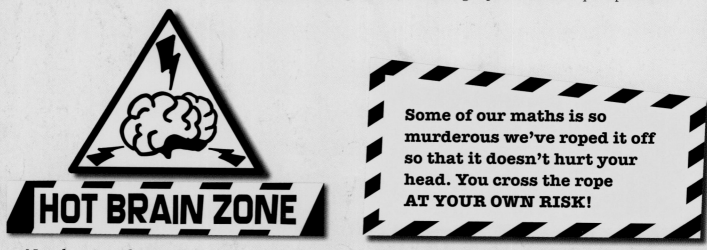

HOT BRAIN ZONE

Some of our maths is so murderous we've roped it off so that it doesn't hurt your head. You cross the rope AT YOUR OWN RISK!

Nearly everything in maths is linked to something else. When you read this book look out for the link signs so you can see how all the different bits join up! ▶ ??

THE MURDEROUS PENNIES

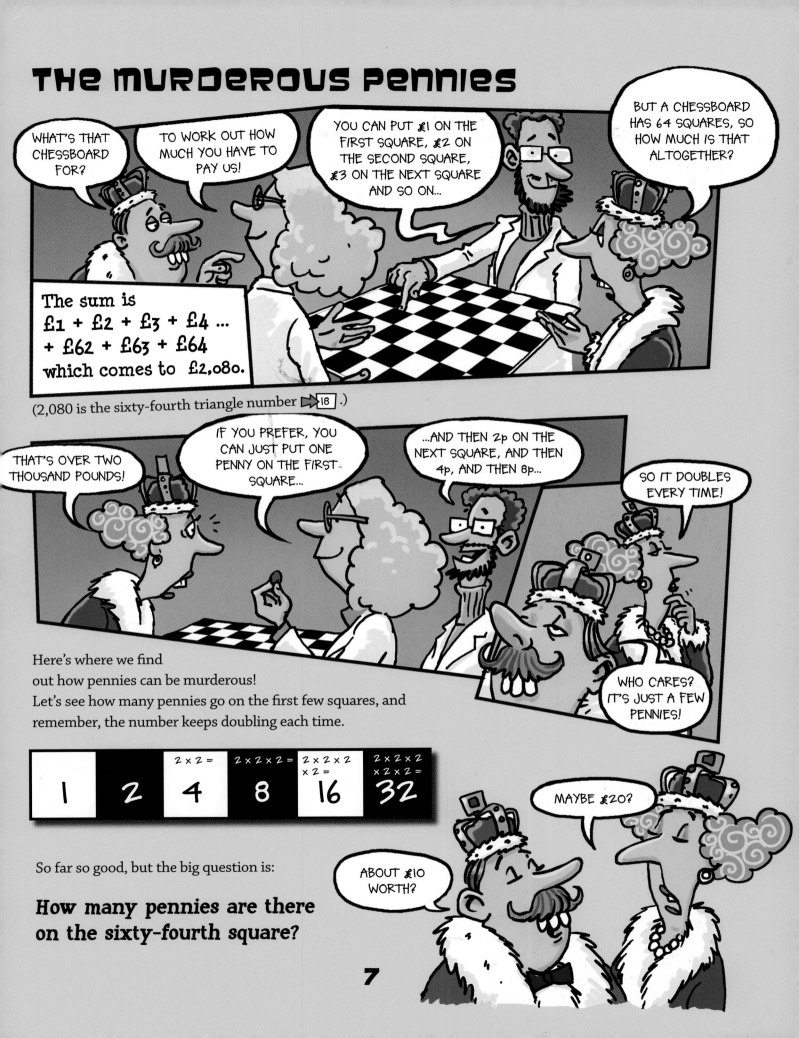

WHAT'S THAT CHESSBOARD FOR?

TO WORK OUT HOW MUCH YOU HAVE TO PAY US!

YOU CAN PUT £1 ON THE FIRST SQUARE, £2 ON THE SECOND SQUARE, £3 ON THE NEXT SQUARE AND SO ON...

BUT A CHESSBOARD HAS 64 SQUARES, SO HOW MUCH IS THAT ALTOGETHER?

The sum is
£1 + £2 + £3 + £4 ...
+ £62 + £63 + £64
which comes to £2,080.

(2,080 is the sixty-fourth triangle number ➡ 18 .)

THAT'S OVER TWO THOUSAND POUNDS!

IF YOU PREFER, YOU CAN JUST PUT ONE PENNY ON THE FIRST SQUARE...

...AND THEN 2p ON THE NEXT SQUARE, AND THEN 4p, AND THEN 8p...

SO IT DOUBLES EVERY TIME!

Here's where we find
out how pennies can be murderous!
Let's see how many pennies go on the first few squares, and
remember, the number keeps doubling each time.

WHO CARES? IT'S JUST A FEW PENNIES!

1	2	$2 \times 2 =$ 4	$2 \times 2 \times 2 =$ 8	$2 \times 2 \times 2 \times 2 =$ 16	$2 \times 2 \times 2 \times 2 \times 2 =$ 32

So far so good, but the big question is:

How many pennies are there on the sixty-fourth square?

ABOUT £10 WORTH?

MAYBE £20?

7

To get the answer you multiply sixty-three 2s together. It's called 2 to the power of 63 and it looks like this:

$$2^{63} = 2×2×2×2×2×2×2×2×2×2×2×2×2×2×2×2×2×2×2×2×2×2×2×2×2×2×2×2×2×2×2×2$$
$$×2×2×2×2×2×2×2×2×2×2×2×2×2×2×2×2×2×2×2×2×2×2×2×2×2×2×2×2×2×2×2$$

The answer is

9,223,372,036,854,775,808 pennies.

THAT'S ABOUT 92 MILLION BILLION POUNDS.

GASP!

HOW BIG WILL THE LAST SQUARE OF THE CHESSBOARD HAVE TO BE?

Suppose your coins are neatly stacked up in a cube shape...

The last square will need to measure about 11·5 miles (18·5 km) along each side, and of course the cube will be 11·5 miles (18·5 km) high. It would be like grabbing all the major cities in the world and making them into a big pile. The pennies would weigh more than 30,000,000,000,000 tonnes, which is a LOT more than the cities.

Height = 11·5 miles

11·5 miles

11·5 miles

Suppose we put all the pennies in one tall thin pile...

The 21st square would have over a million pennies on it and be about a mile (1·6 km) high.
The pennies on the 39th square would reach the moon.
The pennies on the 48th square would go beyond the sun.

NOW THAT'S MURDEROUS!

WHOOMP!

The pile of pennies on the 64th square would be about 1·5 light years high!
(Find out about light years ➡ 92 .)

Numbers don't have to be big to cause trouble. The very smallest numbers might look nice and cute and simple, but sometimes they can be really awkward! That's why we keep them safely locked away down in our Number Vaults. Enter at your own risk...

The Number Vaults

DANGER

Down in the MM vaults we keep all sorts of different numbers. We'll meet some of them in a minute, but first we'd better warn you about the most powerful number of all…

The Evil One!

You might think that the little number 1 can't do anybody any harm, but 1 is the most powerful number of all. All the other numbers are just lots of 1s added together, and you can never ever find the biggest number because you can always add 1 to it and make it even bigger. If you want to see an awesome way of building numbers, look at Pascal's Triangle 72. It starts by adding together a few little 1s and suddenly **WHAM** – it belts out some numbers that are truly murderous!

Shops are helpless without the number 1 because if they haven't got any 1p coins then sometimes they can't give people the exact change.

The Evil One is so powerful that even the Evil Gollarks from the planet Zog are helpless without it.

Somewhere on the other side of outer space…
ZOG BATTLESHIPS
Galaxy Raider
9,999,999q

WE'VE BEEN SAVING UP TO INVADE EARTH!
WE'D LIKE THAT GALAXY RAIDER PLEASE.

SORRY, I'VE ONLY GOT 2q, 5q AND 10q COINS. I CAN'T GIVE YOU THE RIGHT CHANGE.
BAH! WE'LL HAVE TO CANCEL OUR INVASION PLANS!
ALL BECAUSE WE DON'T HAVE A NUMBER 1!

ODDS, EVENS AND A BIT MORE EVILNESS

Odd numbers always end in 1, 3, 5, 7 or 9, and even numbers end in 2, 4, 6, 8 and 0. Adding 1 to an even number immediately changes it to odd and this can give the number 1 a perfect chance to be evil. Out at the tennis club, Pongo McWhiffy has just arrived to find there's an even number of people there including himself. Even numbers always divide exactly by 2 so that means everybody can split into pairs with nobody left out. This is good news for Pongo who has just spotted the terribly lovely Veronica Gumfloss standing alone.

OH NO! ISN'T THERE ANYBODY ELSE I CAN PLAY WITH?

NO, WE'RE THE LAST PAIR, VERONICA!

So far so good for Pongo, but now an Evil One is about to ruin Pongo's day by turning the even number into an odd number.

HI, I JUST GOT HERE. IS THERE SPACE FOR ONE MORE?

OH BOY!

BAH!

If you try to divide an odd number of people into pairs you always get someone left over. Poor old Pongo has been a victim of the Evil One.

10

This is a completely different sort of Evil One... It's our arch enemy Professor Fiendish with one of his diabolical challenges. Watch out, there's sure to be some sneaky trick involved.

- You can have as many turns as you need
- You MUST turn over TWO coins every time
- You can't turn a coin over, then immediately turn it back the next turn*

How diabolical! This puzzle is impossible but can you see why? There are five tails showing. We need to get zero tails showing, but zero is an even number. As long as we can only turn two coins at a time, we can never make the odd number of tails into an even number. If you try this trick on somebody else you can use any number of coins, but make sure you start with an odd number of tails.

How the Evil One can start fights

It's a lovely sunny day **in the Lost Desert** and the vultures are soaring in the sky and happily looking down at stranded snakes baking to death on the rocks. Mungoid the Ungoid has been fixing a snack of turtle tails for himself, Urgum the Axeman and Grizelda the Grisly. All three of them are **ruthless bloodthirsty savages**, so the tails must be shared out absolutely fairly, otherwise there will be a really nasty fight.

When Mungoid divides the tails into three piles, there is exactly the same number in each pile, but then **Hunjah the Headless** turns up, so Mungoid has to divide the tails into four piles. Once again they divide exactly, but then **Jing the Unhinged** appears. Amazingly, the same number of tails divides into five piles so nobody needs to do any fighting.

They are just about to start eating when a spotted turtle rather stupidly wanders past. **WALL-OOCH!** Urgum whacks it with his axe and adds the tail to the feast.

Suddenly the tails won't divide into five equal piles. Immediately everybody reaches for their weapons but then Jing remembers he promised to get some shopping for his mum. Off he goes and Mungoid divides the tails back into four piles – but he can't! With a mighty **YARGGHHHH** Urgum leaps up to attack everybody, but luckily Hunjah realizes that raw turtle tails are actually very disgusting so he goes off to find a raspberry yoghurt instead.

Mungoid divides the tails into three piles again, but he can't make them equal. Urgum's axe is out, **Grizelda has grabbed her sword** and Mungoid has no choice but to reach for his fearsome battle mallet. A peaceful picnic has turned into a battle, and it's all due to the Evil One.

So what happened?

Mungoid started with 60 tails. 60 will divide exactly into three lots of 20. It will also divide into four lots of 15, or five lots of 12. It will also divide by 2, 6, 10 and 30 if you wanted it to. **60 is a friendly and helpful number**, and that's why clocks have 60 seconds in a minute and 60 minutes in an hour.

When Urgum added one more tail, the total number was 61, and 61 is very different from 60! **61 is an awkward prime number**, which means that it won't divide by anything apart from itself and 1. Unless Mungoid had 61 people coming to share the tails, there would always be a fight!

HOW PRIME NUMBERS COULD MAKE YOU FAMOUS FOR EVER!

Prime numbers have been driving people nuts ever since counting was invented. Just outside our Primes Workshop there's a statue of the Ancient Greek who tried to sort them out.

That's odd! Pythagoras died 200 years before Eratosthenes was born. What's his name doing here, and whose are those footprints? We'll catch up with them later but first we've got an invention to show you. It's our own special version of The Sieve of Eratosthenes to find all the primes up to 100.

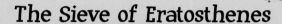

The Sieve of Eratosthenes

1	2	3	4	5	6	7	8	9	10
11	12	13	14	15	16	17	18	19	20
21	22	23	24	25	26	27	28	29	30
31	32	33	34	35	36	37	38	39	40
41	42	43	44	45	46	47	48	49	50
51	52	53	54	55	56	57	58	59	60
61	62	63	64	65	66	67	68	69	70
71	72	73	74	75	76	77	78	79	80
81	82	83	84	85	86	87	88	89	90
91	92	93	94	95	96	97	98	99	100

- ▢ Numbers that divide by 2
- ▢ Numbers that divide by 3
- ▢ Numbers that divide by 5
- ▢ Numbers that divide by 7

(If you're an Eratosthenes fan you can log on to
www.ithinkoldgreekmathsgeeksarewellcoolanddon'tcarewhoknowsitactually.mm.org
or you can just look here ▶ 37 .)

PRIMES WORKSHOP

PYTHAGORAS WAS HERE

ERATOSTHENES OF CYRENE 276–194 BC

We write the numbers out in a square grid and then we work along them one by one. We start with the number 2 and put a green box around it, then we paint every second number green (so that's 4, 6, 8 and so on). We move on to number 3, put a blue box round it and paint every third number blue (so that's 6, 9, 12, 15…) if it hasn't already been painted. When we get to 4 it's already painted so we move on to 5 and paint every fifth number red, then we skip 6 because it's already painted. When we get to 7 we paint every seventh number a lovely shade of damson musk. (Normal books might just use purple, but we like to show how much we care.) When we get to the end of the top line, we can stop. This is the cleverest part of Eratosthenes' system. We've already painted all the numbers up to 100 that will divide up, just leaving the primes!

OI! WHY DID YOU START WITH 2? YOU MISSED ME OUT!

THE EVIL ONE

If we started with number 1 and coloured in all the numbers it divides into, then ALL the numbers would be coloured the same. That wouldn't get us very far! In fact, that's another big stupid pointless argument that's been going on for thousands of years – is the Evil One prime or not?

So far so good, but you'll see that the white boxes with the prime numbers are splattered all over the place! Can you find a way of writing the numbers out so that the primes make a pattern? Any sort of pattern at all? **People are DESPERATE!**

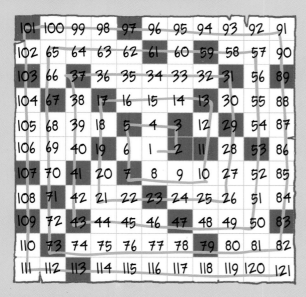

Nobody has managed it yet, but here's one who got close. In 1963, a clever chap called Stanislaw Ulam was doodling away during a meeting. He decided to draw numbers in a spiral and see where the primes turned up. (It must have been a very boring meeting.) A lot of them seemed to land on diagonal lines, which got everybody a bit excited, but as you can see for yourself, it's not brilliant, is it? Even if this diagram had just one continuous line of primes that went on for ever they'd be happy. The line that goes 5, 19, 41, 71, 109 looks promising but if you made the grid bigger, the next number in the line would be 155 which divides by 5.

Go on, have a go! Eratosthenes still gets his name mentioned after 2,000 years, but if you manage to make a pattern out of primes then you'll be remembered for a lot longer.

OT BRAIN ZONE

COULD YOU CRACK A COMPUTER CODE?

We've just multiplied two prime numbers from Eratosthenes' sieve and got 6,497. How quickly could you work out which numbers they are?

Warning: It's tricky! Turn the page to see how computers use prime numbers for codes...

HOW PRIME NUMBERS PAY FOR PIZZAS

You might think prime numbers are just pointless things for people who love sums, but they are very useful for codes. If you multiply two big prime numbers together and give somebody the answer, it's very hard to work out what the two primes were.

When Veronica sends her credit card number over the internet, her computer keeps the number secret with a system that multiplies two prime numbers that are hundreds of digits long.

Pongo's computer knows how to decode the number, but if anyone else wants to steal Veronica's credit card details they'll need to work out what the two prime numbers were. Even with the best computers it could take thousands of years!

COMPUTER CODE ANSWER:

73 × 89 = 6,497
THINK HOW LONG IT WOULD HAVE TAKEN TO WORK OUT IF WE'D USED MASSIVE PRIME NUMBERS!

How a Prime number can stop you from Being eaten

If you're wondering why we keep a sleeping bug in our Number Vaults, this is no ordinary bug, it's a North American cicada. It might only be about the size of your finger but it is one of the cleverest creatures to use prime numbers on the planet.

The cicadas live underground and come out once every 17 years. One major swarm came out in May 2004. They spent a few weeks singing loudly and laying eggs, then they dropped dead. Before that, they were out in 1987 and they'll be back in 2021. The amazing thing is that the 17-year gap is no accident. It stops them getting eaten!

Suppose there was a natural predator which had a life-cycle of three years, and they depended on eating cicadas for the first year of their life. If the cicadas appeared every 6 years, then every second generation of predators would be able to rely on eating them. Good news for the predators, but bad news for the cicadas.

What if the cicadas didn't use a prime number? Suppose their cycle was every 10 years, then a predator with either a 2-year or 5-year life cycle could rely upon them within a reasonable number of generations. That's why the cicadas rather cleverly picked quite a large prime number of years between appearances. Unless a predator had a 17-year life cycle, it can't rely on the cicadas. And predators simply can't be bothered to wait 17 years!

The cicadas are right to be careful because they are low-fat, full of protein and taste OK. There are lots of other sorts of cicadas, including one type that has a 13-year cycle.

CREEPY CICADA FACTS

At the peak of the 2004 swarming season...

- There were about 10,000,000,000,000 cicadas – that's 1,500 for every human on earth.

- Their combined weight was almost double the weight of the entire population of the US.

- They produced enough poo to fill 300 Olympic-sized swimming pools every day.

- There were about 25 cicadas for every square metre! They completely covered trees, bushes, parks, etc.

- They left behind about 500 trillion eggs. Somebody calculated that in a single square mile of forest there could be as many eggs as there are stars in the Milky Way.

A 2,500-year-old murder mystery

THE STORY STARTS IN HERE.

Triangle and Square Numbers

Remember those footprints we saw earlier? The great detective Sheerluck Homes has picked up the trail and he's followed it into one of the darkest corners of our basement. He's trying to sort out the mystery of a murder that happened 2,500 years ago.

If you get a load of coins (or counters or cannonballs or anything else), you can arrange them into triangle shapes of different sizes. The numbers of coins you need for each shape are the triangle numbers. (The first triangle number only has one coin so it isn't much of a triangle.) The fifth triangle is exactly the same pattern you use if you're setting the balls up for a game of pool.

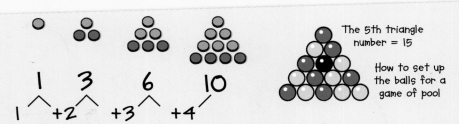

The 5th triangle number = 15

How to set up the balls for a game of pool

1   3   6   10

1 ^ +2 ^ +3 ^ +4

You can see how all the triangle numbers mysteriously appear in Pascal's Triangle ➡ 79 .

To get all the TRIANGLE NUMBERS you start with 1 then add 2, add 3, add 4 ... and keep going!

Now we're going to put the coins into squares. You can make square numbers by multiplying a number by itself. We show this with a little 2, e.g. $3^2 = 3 \times 3 = 9$

$1^2=1$ $2^2=4$ $3^2=9$ $4^2=16$

1 ^ +3 ^ +5 ^ +7

To get all the SQUARE NUMBERS you start with 1 then add 3, add 5, add 7 ... and keep going!

THIS MIGHT SEEM ALL VERY SWEET, BUT SOON YOU'LL SEE HOW SOMEBODY GETS MURDERED ON A BOAT!

The first clue!

AT FIRST I THOUGHT THERE WAS NOTHING STRANGE ABOUT NUMBERS UNTIL I DISCOVERED THIS TRICK...

1. Arrange coins to make ANY triangle or square number.
2. Remove 2 coins.
3. You'll NEVER be able to divide the rest of the coins into exactly three lots.

21 − 2 = 19
This won't divide by 3

16 − 2 = 14
This won't divide by 3

You can try this, or better still try it on your friends. They'll spend ages trying to find a square or triangle number that works, but there isn't one!

THAT'S WHEN I REALIZED NUMBERS COULD DRIVE A MAN TO KILL!

HOW DID NUMBERS LEAD TO MURDER?

Some people think that they should be able to make simple numbers do anything they like. When they find that the numbers refuse to play, they get very very cross! Here's the problem that caused the trouble:

If you take ANY square number and double it, you cannot get another square number.

For instance if we add two lots of 5^2, we almost get 7^2...

...but we can't get it exactly!

Pythagoras of Samos was one of the first and biggest maths stars ever. He died back in 475 BC so it's a bit strange to find him running around and sticking his nose in. (Mind you he was a strange guy. He used to have a whole gang of followers who worshipped numbers, and their religion didn't let them eat beans.)

5^2 5^2 7^2

There's an EVIL ONE left over!

DON'T REMIND ME!

GOOD GRIEF, IT'S MY PRIME SUSPECT!

BEGONE!

THAT'S A GOOD THROW FOR A DEAD PERSON!

THIS EVIL ONE RUINED EVERYTHING FOR ME!

WHAT A FUNNY-LOOKING COIN!

Oh dear! You can guess where this is going...

SO WHY DID DOUBLING SQUARES UPSET YOU SO MUCH?

IT GAVE ME A SUM I COULDN'T SOLVE.

Somewhere far, far away

IT'S A 1q COIN! I CAN GIVE YOU CHANGE NOW.

HURRAH! NOW WE CAN INVADE EARTH.

PLINK!

I'LL GO AND PACK SOME SANDWICHES.

PYTHAGORAS' MURDEROUS RULE

Pythagoras liked to think he could solve any problem in maths, and the most famous bit of maths he did involved right-angled triangles. A right angle is the same shape as the corner of a square and we usually mark it with a little square shape.

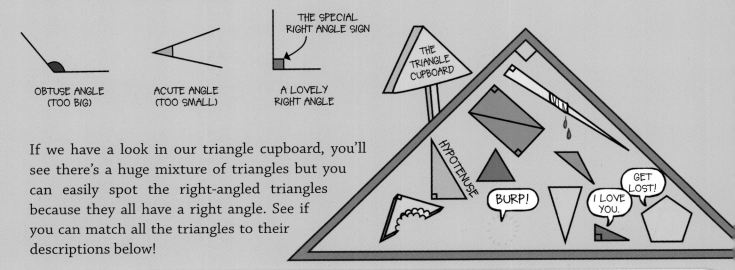

OBTUSE ANGLE (TOO BIG)

ACUTE ANGLE (TOO SMALL)

THE SPECIAL RIGHT ANGLE SIGN

A LOVELY RIGHT ANGLE

THE TRIANGLE CUPBOARD

HYPOTENUSE

BURP!

I LOVE YOU.

GET LOST!

If we have a look in our triangle cupboard, you'll see there's a huge mixture of triangles but you can easily spot the right-angled triangles because they all have a right angle. See if you can match all the triangles to their descriptions below!

1. **A** right-angled triangle with a label telling you that the longest side is called the hypotenuse.

2. **A** scalene triangle – all the sides are different lengths.

3. **An** isosceles triangle without a right angle. Isosceles means that two sides are the same length.

4. **An** isosceles triangle with a right angle. (Clue: this triangle is far bigger than any of the others!)

5. **An** invisible triangle with bad manners.

6. **A** right-angled sandwich triangle.

7. **A** very long thin right-angled triangle that's had an accident.

8. Two matching right-angled triangles making a rectangle.

9. **An** equilateral triangle – this has all three sides the same length.

10. **A** teeny little right-angled triangle that fancies a pentagon.

As you can see, triangles can be a bit mad but Pythagoras worked out a rule that ALL right-angled triangles have to obey!

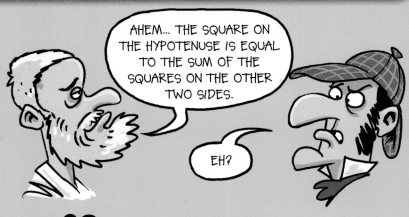

AHEM... THE SQUARE ON THE HYPOTENUSE IS EQUAL TO THE SUM OF THE SQUARES ON THE OTHER TWO SIDES.

EH?

It sounds a bit confusing, but it's easy to test. If a triangle has sides measuring 3 cm, 4 cm and 5 cm then it will have a right angle. We'll draw this triangle out, then put a big square on each side. We can divide the three big squares into lots of little squares and see what happens.

Pythagoras said that the square on the longest side of a right-angled triangle always has to be the same size as the squares on the two other sides added together. You can check this one yourself, either by counting up all the little squares or using the numbers.

This rule is called **Pythagoras' Theorem**, and sets of numbers that make right-angled triangles such as 3-4-5 are called **Pythagorean triples**.

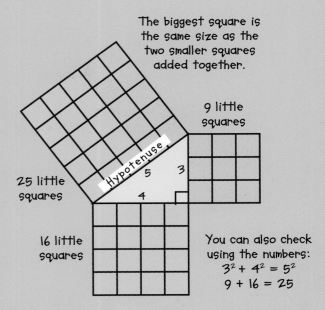

The biggest square is the same size as the two smaller squares added together.

9 little squares

25 little squares

16 little squares

You can also check using the numbers:
$3^2 + 4^2 = 5^2$
$9 + 16 = 25$

HOW TO MAKE YOUR VERY OWN PYTHAGOREAN TRIPLE

1. Pick ANY odd number. This will be the short side of your triangle. Divide a big square into little squares with your chosen number of squares along each side.

We've picked 7.

2. Split the square into two bits so that one bit has one more square than the other.

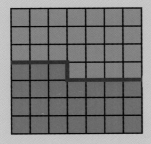

3. Count the squares in each bit to get the other two numbers for your right-angled triangle!

25

7

24

4. If you don't believe it could be so simple – test your numbers!

$7^2 + 24^2 = 25^2$
$49 + 576 = 625$

(You can also make triples using the Fibonacci Series 58 .)

BUT HOW DID YOUR FAMOUS THEOREM LEAD YOU TO MURDER?

EVERYTHING WAS FINE UNTIL THAT FATEFUL AFTERNOON ABOUT 2,500 YEARS AGO...

THANKS FOR INVITING US TO YOUR BOAT PARTY, PYTHAGORAS.

HIPPASUS HAS GOT A PROBLEM FOR YOU.

HOW LONG'S THE HYPOTENUSE IF BOTH THE SHORT SIDES MEASURE 1?

THAT SOUNDS FUN!

Pythagoras knew the answer had to be somewhere between 1 and 2 but he couldn't work it out exactly. (And the answer is not 1·5! You'll see why later.)

If this side was 1 it would be TOO SHORT for this corner to be a right angle.
1
1
1
If this side was 2 then it would be TOO LONG! The triangle would have to be stretched out flat to join the sides up.
2
1 1

What was worse, he found that if he had ANY right-angled triangle with two sides the same length, he couldn't work out the third side!

This is because if you double a square number you can never get another square number. (Did you remember that? 19)

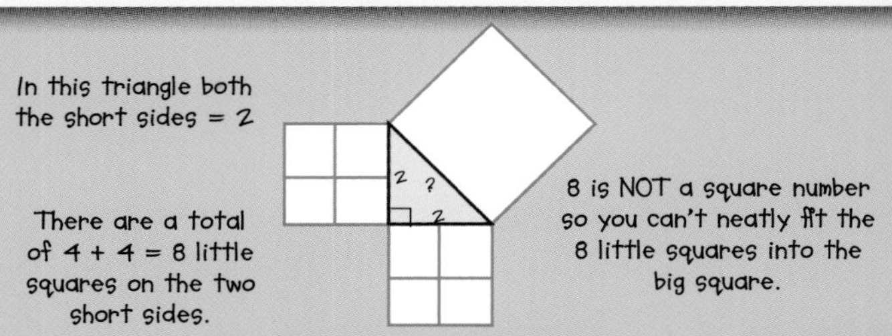
In this triangle both the short sides = 2
There are a total of 4 + 4 = 8 little squares on the two short sides.
2
?
2
8 is NOT a square number so you can't neatly fit the 8 little squares into the big square.

...AND WHEN PYTHAGORAS REALIZED HE COULDN'T GET AN EXACT ANSWER...
WAIT TILL WE GET BACK AND I TELL EVERYBODY YOU CAN'T SORT OUT THIS LITTLE TRIANGLE!
IF HIPPASUS TELLS EVERYBODY THEN I'M RUINED!
SO NO MORE BOAT PARTIES?
THEN WE'D BETTER KEEP HIM QUIET, HADN'T WE?

Here's the answer that killed Hippasus...

HEY PYTHO, WHERE'S HIPPASUS?
HE'S FEEDING THE FISH.
HO HO!
AND THAT'S THE TRUE STORY OF ONE OF THE MOST MURDEROUS BITS OF MATHS!

HOT BRAIN ZONE

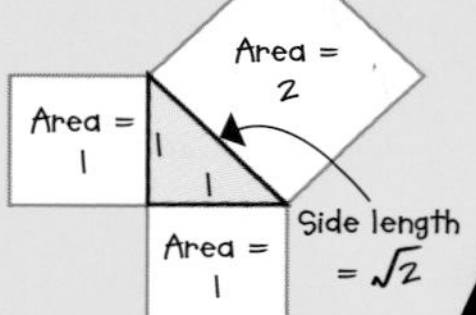
Area = 2
Area = 1
1
1
Area = 1
Side length = √2

If we draw out Hippasus' little triangle, Pythagoras' theorem tells us that the area of the square on the hypotenuse is 1+1 = 2. To find the length of the side of the square we need to know what number multiplied by itself makes 2. This is called the square root of two and we write it like this: $\sqrt{2}$

If you try this on a calculator you get 1·414213562373...

The everlasting birthday

Many famous people have tried to change the progress of time. What follows is the report of one such attempt that had been long forgotten until we discovered it in some old police files...

City: Chicago, Illinois USA
Place: Luigi's Diner, Upper Main St

Date: 3 June 1931
Time: 2:00 p.m.

Lunchtime was over and the dustbin behind the counter was overflowing with coloured ribbons, dainty envelopes and fancy wrapping paper. Benni the waiter scraped a bowl of leftover spaghetti sauce over the top then looked around the room to see how many customers were left. As usual it was just the one group with nowhere better to go. Benni knew it was dangerous to try and hurry them. All he could do was hope that they wouldn't cause trouble.

I GUESS THAT'S IT FOR ANOTHER YEAR THEN.

Dolly Snowlips looked round at the seven shady men sitting with her around the centre table. They shifted uncomfortably in their suits.

"So do you like the birthday present I got you Dolly?" asked the man in the blackest suit. "It's poyf-yoom."

"Sure, Blade," said Dolly. She picked up a little fancy bottle from the table and read the label. "Midnight Daisy Perfume. Real thoughtful."

"That's good," said Blade Boccelli. "I hoped it'd be a surprise."

"It was a surprise, that's for sure."

"How about my present?" said all the others. "Was it a surprise?"

"Let me see now," said Dolly checking all the other little bottles lined up in front of her. "Perfume, perfume, perfume, perfume, perfume and perfume. I got seven bottles of perfume. Yeah, I guess you can say I was surprised."

GREAT!

"Great?" snapped Dolly. "You guys must think I stink real bad if I need seven bottles!" Dolly slammed the bottle she was holding down on the table so hard that it smashed. The door behind the counter flew open, knocking Benni head first into the bin. Luigi the restaurant owner dashed out.

"What's going on?" he shouted. "I thought I heard a shot! I told you guys, no shooting until you've paid the bill."

"Sorry Luigi," said Dolly. "That wasn't no shooting, I just got cross."

"I don't blame you," said Luigi, sniffing the air. "I'd be cross too if I was sitting with a bunch of guys who all smelt like Midnight Daisies."

"It's Miss Snowlips' birthday," said a mouth that was full of pretty ribbons and cold spaghetti sauce.

I KNOW THAT!

Luigi looked at Benni's legs, which were sticking up out of the dustbin. "And I've got a surprise for her."

"Oh no!" shouted the seven shady men all getting up and backing away from Dolly. "Don't give her poyf-yoom!"

"Perfume? No, it's a cake. I'll bring it out just as soon as I've said goodnight to my mom." Luigi disappeared into the back room.

"Come and sit down again guys," said Dolly. Slowly they all crept back to their seats. "I know you tried your best, but this birthday thing gets me down."

"I love birthdays," said the biggest man.

Porky Boccelli tucked a napkin into his collar and licked his lips.

IT MAKES A CHANGE TO HAVE CAKE AFTER LUNCH.

"So what do you usually have after lunch?" asked Chainsaw Charlie.

"He usually has more lunch after lunch," sneered Half-Smile Gabrianni.

"I heard that!" shouted Porky while pulling a sharpened pickle fork out of a secret pocket in his hat. Charlie leapt to his feet and tugged a chainsaw from his sleeve while Half-Smile whipped out his high-velocity catapult.

DROP IT, BOYS!

One-Finger Jimmy reached for his gun. Jimmy might only have had one finger, but it could pull a trigger mighty fast. They all dropped it. "This is Dolly's birthday and she's being miserable about it so show some respect. We got to be miserable too."

"Thank you, Jimmy," said Dolly. "But the birthday isn't so bad. It's just that night-time comes, and then it's the next day and then there's no more birthday and I'm just one lousy year older. I wish my birthday could go on for ever."

The men around the table all nodded. "If there was a way we could fix that for you, we'd fix it," said Blade. "But we'd need to stop the night-time coming."

"Just a minute!" said Weasel, the smallest man. "Luigi went to say goodnight to his mom and it's only lunchtime. How does that work?"

"He's on the phone," explained Benni who had pulled himself out of the bin and was now scooping spaghetti sauce out of his ear with a spoon. "She lives in Europe and it's nearly night-time there."

"You mean they have night at lunchtime?" gasped Porky.

"Why not?" sneered Half-Smile Gabrianni. "After all, some days you're still eating your lunch at night-time."

IT'S TO DO WITH THE WAY THE WORLD SPINS ROUND AND WHERE THE SUN SHINES.

Benni spat out a strand of spaghetti. "Some folks have daytime while other folks have night-time."

Blade clicked his fingers. "Benni, you're a genius!" he grinned. "I just figured out how Dolly can have an everlasting birthday! Get me a melon, some cocktail umbrellas and a lamp."

AND THIS IS GOING TO GIVE ME A BIRTHDAY THAT LASTS FOR EVER?

IF BLADE'S GONNA TELL US ONE OF HIS WACKO IDEAS, IT'LL JUST SEEM LIKE IT LASTS FOR EVER.

Soon Blade had stuck four cocktail umbrellas in the melon and made a plan on the table to show how daytime and night-time work.

"The melon is the earth and this is how it would look if we were floating a few trillion miles above the North Pole. The light from the sun can only shine on half the planet at a time. The four cocktail sticks represent four guys, and as the melon spins round they get moved into the light and then out of it again."

What happens when the earth spins round as explained by B Boccelli

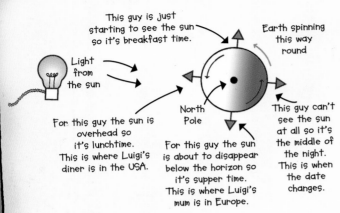

This guy is just starting to see the sun so it's breakfast time.

Earth spinning this way round

Light from the sun

North Pole

For this guy the sun is overhead so it's lunchtime. This is where Luigi's diner is in the USA.

For this guy the sun is about to disappear below the horizon so it's supper time. This is where Luigi's mum is in Europe.

This guy can't see the sun at all so it's the middle of the night. This is when the date changes.

"That's all very well, Blade," said Weasel. "But if we're going to stop the night coming and the date changing, we need to stop the earth moving round."

"I don't believe this," muttered Dolly. "Blade promises to make the earth stop moving for me."

"No I don't," said Blade. He pulled a toy car out of his pocket and held it against the melon. "We keep you moving one way while the world turns the other way. That way you'll stay in the sunlight. Night-time will never arrive and the next day will never come!"

If the car keeps moving fast enough it will always stay in the sunlight!

Blade looked around proudly. Every jaw was hanging open in astonishment. "Speechless, huh?" he said.

Blade thought it was because his plan was so brilliant but actually it was because they

were wondering why he'd had a toy car in his pocket. Eventually Dolly spoke. "Blade, can't you see a problem with this driving round the world thing?"

"Like what?"

"Like crossing mountains, deserts and oceans?"

"Yeah, but apart from that it's foolproof! All we have to do is keep following the sun. It'll never be dark so the day will never end so your birthday will last for ever!"

GEE WHIZZ!

"So you're saying that if you set off now and go round the world and get back in 24 hours' time, it'll still be 3 June for you? But for Benni waiting here it'll be 4 June?"

"Sure! If we never see night-time, why not?" said Porky. "Blade just invented time travel."

"It's just too crazy," said Dolly trying to think it out. "If you kept on going, you'd be stuck on 3 June 1931 with those spaghetti stains on your tie for ever. Everybody else would be like spaceman people in the future with earrings in their noses and talking into teeny little telephones that don't need wires."

"Ha ha!" laughed Blade. "Phones without wires? Now you're the one being crazy!"

IS THE EVERLASTING BIRTHDAY POSSIBLE?

If you enjoy your birthday, you might like to try Blade's plan yourself. Obviously we don't recommend you drive because it's far easier to fly round the world.

WHY IS THAT BIRTHDAY CAKE SO BIG?

IT'S GOT TO LAST FOR EVER!

The big question is how fast you need to go to keep up with the sun. If you were going to fly right around the equator, the total distance is about 25,000 miles. As the Earth spins round once every 24 hours, that's how long you've got, so your speed would need to be 25,000 ÷ 24 = about 1,040 miles per hour. Most cars start to make strange noises and smell funny if you do more than 100 miles per hour so this is another reason why we don't suggest you drive.

If you set off from anywhere that's not on the equator then you don't need to go so far or so fast.

If you keep going round the world at the right speed then Blade is right, you'll never have night-time. But suppose Blade and the gang tried it and got back to Luigi's 24 hours later. Would it still be 3 June for them and 4 June for Benni?

The answer is no, because of the International Date Line. This is a long line drawn on maps of the world that goes from the North Pole down to the South Pole. It mainly runs through the Pacific Ocean, and there are a few bends in it so that it doesn't divide up countries or groups of islands that want to be together.

International Date Line

west ← → east

When you cross the date line heading west, it doesn't matter what time it is, the date moves on one day. For Blade it'll go from 3 June to 4 June so he can't make Dolly's birthday last for ever.

Chasing the Sun

(How far and how fast you have to go in 24 hours approximately!)

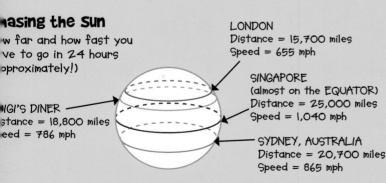

LUIGI'S DINER
Distance = 18,800 miles
Speed = 786 mph

LONDON
Distance = 15,700 miles
Speed = 655 mph

SINGAPORE
(almost on the EQUATOR)
Distance = 25,000 miles
Speed = 1,040 mph

SYDNEY, AUSTRALIA
Distance = 20,700 miles
Speed = 865 mph

BUT YOU CAN MAKE YOUR BIRTHDAY TWICE AS LONG...

If you cross the date line heading east then the date moves back one day!

The stretch of sea between America and Russia is called the Bering Strait. The narrowest bit is about 50 miles wide and there are two tiny islands in it that are two miles apart. These are the Diomede Islands and the date line passes in between them. You start your birthday on Big Diomede, then just as your birthday is ending at midnight, you sail across to Little Diomede and the same date starts again!

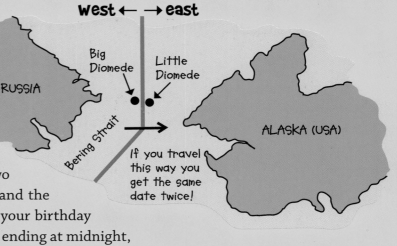

Meanwhile out on the highway heading west...

"Faster, Jimmy!" said Blade. "Faster, faster!" The rest of the men were wedged into the back seat of the Dodge Sedan as Jimmy jammed his foot to the floor and the car screamed down the highway.

"Shame Dolly didn't come with us," shouted Porky over the noise. "I thought we were doing this for her."

"She said it wouldn't work!" sulked Blade. "Well we'll show her. Hey Numbers, did you figure out how fast we have to go yet?"

The nervous thin man in the back of the car checked the scribbles he'd made on his shirt cuff. "I make it 786 miles per hour!"

"We'll never do it, Blade," said Weasel.

"Sure we will!" said Blade. "What's going to stop us?"

"THAT!" said Jimmy, slamming on the brakes.

Blade looked ahead to see a solid wall of police cars parked across the road. With a screech of rubber the car skidded to a halt and before they knew it they had all been dragged out and lined up. The officer in charge came over and stared Blade in the eye.

"Do you know what speed you were going?" said Lieutenant Ptchowsky.

"Ninety-two," said Blade.

"Ninety-two?" gasped Lieutenant Ptchowsky. "The limit here's 40. What were you trying to do?"

"We were trying to do 786," said Blade.

Lieutenant Ptchowsky reached for the handcuffs. "Well now you'll have to do something different," he laughed. "You'll do six months in Grimstate Jail!"

The three oldest problems in the world...
finally solved with a bit of
Murderous Maths!

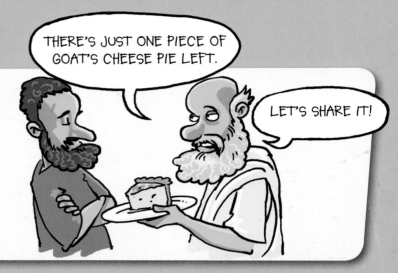

We've already met a couple of the ancient Greek maths celebrities, but back in those days almost anybody with half a brain was having a go. They especially liked playing around with shapes such as circles and triangles and cubes, but they came up against three basic jobs that they couldn't do. We've got a few more ancient Greeks having a tea break in our Geometry Zone, so let's see what they're up to.

Whenever the Greeks did things like dividing a piece of pie up, they liked to do it absolutely exactly. Unfortunately they didn't make life easy for themselves because they were only allowed to use two items:

They had lots of strict rules, but the main ones were...

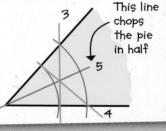

Straight edge   Compasses

Luckily it's easy to divide the piece of pie into two. All the Greeks need to do is bisect the angle, which means to chop it in half.

First we draw two curves with the compasses...

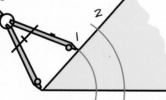

...and then use the straight edge to draw these three lines.

This line chops the pie in half

So far so good, but here's where the trouble starts.

To divide the pie exactly into three, the Greeks need to trisect the angle and they never found a way of doing it using their compasses and straight edge. But we like a bit of a challenge at Murderous Maths, so here we go!

HOW TO TRISECT an angle

NOT!

All we need are two identical rulers that don't have the ends chewed.

OI! NO MEASURING ALLOWED!

What's his problem? We're not going to do any measuring.

First we lie a ruler against one edge of the pie and draw a line parallel to it.

OBJECTION!

HOW GHASTLY!

Now we put the two rulers together so that the ends are exactly in line, then we lie them on the pie like this. (It takes a bit of fiddling about to get them in exactly the right place.)

OI! NO FIDDLING ABOUT!

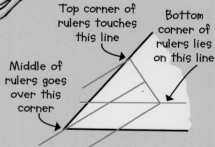

Top corner of rulers touches this line

Bottom corner of rulers lies on this line

Middle of rulers goes over this corner

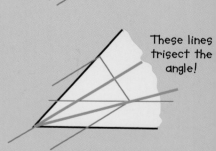

These lines trisect the angle!

All we need to do now is draw in the two lines shown here in green. There, we've just shown how to divide the piece of pie into three equal bits.

Trisecting an angle is known as one of the **Three Unsolved Problems of Antiquity** but as we've just solved it, let's keep a score.

MURDEROUS MATHS 1 : ANCIENT GREEKS 0

OK, maybe we did cheat a bit, but now let's see if we can sort out the other two. That'll really upset the Greeks!

HOW TO SQUARE A CIRCLE

NOT!

The problem is that you start with a circle and you have to draw a square with exactly the same area. The key to this problem is π.

THAT'S ONE OF OUR GREEK LETTERS AND WE CALL IT PI.

If you measure the circumference of any circle and divide it by the diameter you get 3·14159265358 97932384626433832795 ... and this long decimal goes on for ever without making any sort of pattern so usually we just write π.

$$\frac{Circumference}{Diameter} = \pi = 3.14159265...$$

THE π PERSONALITY TEST

Lots of people try to remember as many digits of π as they can. You can tell what kind of a person **YOU** are by how much of π you know.

π = **3** or **4** You're reading the wrong book, but thanks for looking in.

π = **3·14** Very sensible. Your sums will be accurate to **1** in **2,000**.

π = **3·1416** Clever without getting silly. You're a cool operator.

π = **3·14159265** Now you're getting a bit flash, but your friends might be impressed.

π = **3·14159265358979** Brilliant, but it's probably best not to mention this to your friends if you still have any.

π = the first **100** digits Ignore what people say and be proud. There's even a special π club you can join.

π = the first **100,000** digits (the world record) You're reading the wrong book, but thanks for looking in.

If you're trying to convert anything straight such as a line or a square into a circle then π gets involved somewhere.

The Greeks' problem was that they wanted to draw a straight line that was exactly as long as the circumference of a circle. It's impossible with a pair of compasses and a straight edge, but fortunately the Murderous Maths Organization has a fantastically brilliant piece of highly sophisticated equipment that can do it. We'll just go to the canteen and get it out of the cupboard.

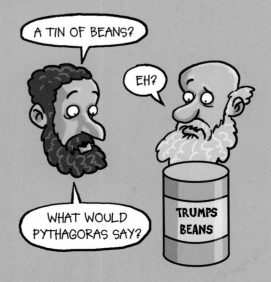

A TIN OF BEANS?

EH?

WHAT WOULD PYTHAGORAS SAY?

TRUMPS BEANS

Here's how to use our tin of beans to draw a length of π.

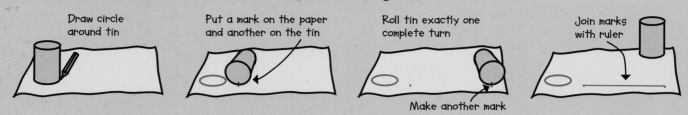

Draw circle around tin

Put a mark on the paper and another on the tin

Roll tin exactly one complete turn

Make another mark

Join marks with ruler

We've just got one more job to do. We need to draw in the diameter of the circle. The Greeks had their own posh way of doing it, but we've got a quick way that uses anything with a right-angled corner – such as a piece of paper or even this book!

HOW TO FIND A DIAMETER WITH A BOOK

1. Put a corner on the edge

2. Mark where the edges cross

2

3. Remove the book

4. Join the marks

THAT BREAKS THE RULES TOO!

BUT IT'S CLEVER.

This works because any triangle that has all three corners on a circle and uses a diameter as one side will have an angle of 90°.

So far we've got a circle with a diameter and a straight line. If we say the diameter of our circle measures 1, then the length of the line is π.

THAT IS SO AWESOME.

I WISH WE COULD HAVE DRAWN THAT!

π

1

This diagram of the circle and the π line might look a bit boring, but the Greeks would have thought it was totally brilliant because they had no way of drawing it using their strict rules. That's a pity because if they had got this far, they had ways to make the line into a square with the same area as the circle. (You can see how at www.murderousmaths.co.uk) Let's check the score so far...

MURDEROUS MATHS 2 : ANCIENT GREEKS 0

Wahey! Two down and one to go, so now let's see if we can sort out the last of the Three Unsolved Problems of Antiquity.

DOUBLING THE CUBE

Legend has it that it took the Greeks 80 years to work out how to exactly double the volume of their altar, and even then they had to relax their rules a bit. (The plague had already died out by then.) But why was it so difficult?

To keep the sums simple we'll imagine the altar is a cube measuring 1 along each side. If you multiply the sides together you get the volume, so $1 \times 1 \times 1 = 1$.

Volume = $1 \times 1 \times 1 = 1$

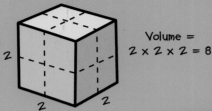

Volume = $2 \times 2 \times 2 = 8$

When the Greeks doubled the length of each side, the volume became $2 \times 2 \times 2 = 8$. This is the same as eight of the small altars put together which was far too big!

THE ORACLE SAID WE HAD TO DOUBLE THE VOLUME.

TRY AGAIN JUST DOUBLING ONE OF THE SIDES.

OK.

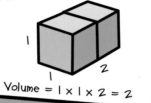

IF YOU JUST DOUBLE THE LENGTH OF ONE SIDE YOU WILL GET A VOLUME OF 2, BUT THE SHAPE STOPS BEING A CUBE. THAT'S NO GOOD IF YOU WANT YOUR GODS TO GET RID OF A PLAGUE THAT'S KILLING EVERYBODY.

Volume = $1 \times 1 \times 2 = 2$

OH NO! THAT'S MADE THEM CROSSER THAN EVER!

IT HAS TO BE EXACTLY THE SAME SHAPE, JUST TWICE THE VOLUME.

SUPPOSE I MAKE THE SIDES' LENGTH $1\frac{1}{2}$?

HOW'S THAT?

VOLUME = $1\frac{1}{2} \times 1\frac{1}{2} \times 1\frac{1}{2} = 3.375$

NOT BAD.

TOO BIG!

I'LL TRY SIDES OF $1\frac{1}{4}$.

VERY SLIGHTLY TOO SMALL.

SO SHOW ME, EXACTLY HOW LONG SHOULD THE SIDES BE?

THAT'S THE TRICKY BIT!

The Greeks needed to know what length multiplied by itself three times made 2. This length is called the cube root of 2 which we can write as $\sqrt[3]{2}$. If you work this out on a calculator you get 1·25992104989487316476721031c... Yes, it's one of those numbers you can't actually write out! But can you draw it?

Here's the problem...

HOW TO TURN THIS	INTO THIS
1	$\sqrt[3]{2}$

And if you're ready to enter a hot brain zone, we'll give you the answer that would have saved the Greeks years and years of plague.

HOT BRAIN ZONE

HOW TO DRAW $\sqrt[3]{2}$

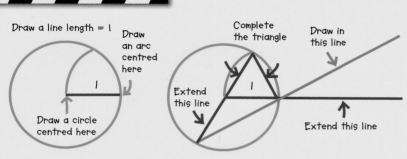

So far we've just used the compasses and straight edge, but here's the dodgy bit.

Mark a length of 'l' on the straight edge

Once you've got your straight edge marked, you have to put it on the drawing and fiddle it around until you get it in exactly the right place.

YOU'RE NOT ALLOWED TO MARK THE STRAIGHT EDGE!

THIS IS NO TIME TO BE FUSSY! WE'RE TRYING TO CURE THE PLAGUE.

OOOH, YOU'VE GOT SOME NASTY SPOTS!

Move straight edge into position. It must touch top of triangle

The 'l' mark is on this line

The end sits on this line

Draw this line

Finally this is what you end up with. The builder can then take his measurement from the diagram and make an altar that's exactly the right size. But for some people, it's too late.

HERE LIES A GREEK THE PLAGUE WIPED OUT, FOR HE REFUSED TO FIDDLE ABOUT.

Once the Greeks relaxed their rules they found several other ways to solve their cube-doubling problem, but with just compasses and a straight edge they had no chance.

MURDEROUS MATHS 3 : ANCIENT GREEKS 0

Infinite flowers and exact eggs

SO NO MEASURING! AND NO PROTRACTORS!

AND NO FIDDLING ABOUT!

Before we leave the Geometry Zone, let's see some of the shapes the Greeks *could* draw just using their straight edge and compasses.

THE PERILOUS PURPLE LOOSESTRIFE

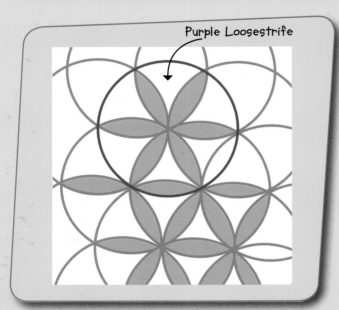

Purple Loosestrife

This is very important.

1. Draw a circle and then make sure you don't adjust your compasses even a tiny bit.

2. Stick the compass point on the edge of the first circle and draw another circle.

3. Stick the compass point in where the circles cross and draw another circle.

4. Repeat **3.**

5. Repeat **4.**

6. Repeat **3.** and **4.** and **5.** until the whole world is covered in purple flowers. Wow yeah, groovy baby.

In case anybody asks you what sort of flower this is supposed to be, you can say it's the six-petalled purple loosestrife. Each plant can produce about 2,500,000 tiny seeds every year, and they spread around very easily. Once they take root they are difficult to get out, so maybe they really will take over the whole world one day!

EQUILATERAL TRIANGLE

Grab a purple loosestrife and join up the ends of three petals.

HEXAGON

Join up all six petals of a purple loosestrife. Hah! That'll teach them that they can't take over the world.

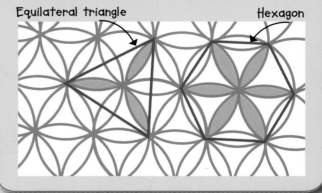

Equilateral triangle

Hexagon

HEY – INVADING EARTH IS OUR JOB!

TOUGH LUCK, WE'RE ALREADY THERE!

an easy trick that's hard to say

Before we look at other shapes, you need to know one of the easiest tricks in maths. It's the 'how to chop a line in half at 90°' trick or if you're feeling posh you say 'how to construct a **perpendicular bisector**'. By the time you've read this, you could have already done it!

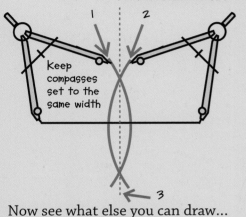

How to construct a
PERPENDICULAR BISECTOR

keep compasses set to the same width

Now see what else you can draw...

HOW TO DRAW an EGG

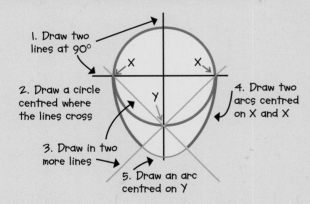

1. Draw two lines at 90°

2. Draw a circle centred where the lines cross

3. Draw in two more lines

4. Draw two arcs centred on X and X

5. Draw an arc centred on Y

FOR THE PERFECT PENTAGON KEEP YOUR COMPASSES SET EXACTLY THE SAME FOR ALL THE CIRCLES AND ARCS.

TO DRAW TWO LINES AT 90°, FIRST DRAW ONE LINE THEN DRAW A PERPENDICULAR BISECTOR.

ERATOSTHENES' EARTH

The Greeks managed to work out the most amazing things with their drawings. Do you remember Eratosthenes with his prime numbers? He was also the first person to work out the size of the Earth using geometry.

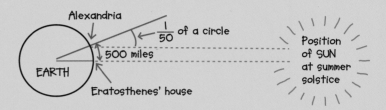

Alexandria

$\frac{1}{50}$ of a circle

500 miles

EARTH

Position of SUN at summer solstice

Eratosthenes' house

Eratosthenes reckoned that the sun was directly over his house in Egypt during the summer solstice. At the same time it was 1/50th of a circle (about 7.2°) from being directly above the city of Alexandria, which he estimated was about 500 miles due north. He decided that 500 miles was therefore 1/50th of the Earth's circumference, and so the circumference of the Earth was 500 × 50 = 25,000 miles or about 40,000 km. This is an extremely close answer but it was also rather lucky!

It turns out that the sun wasn't directly overhead, Alexandria wasn't directly north and it wasn't exactly 500 miles away!

HOW TO DRAW a PENTAGON

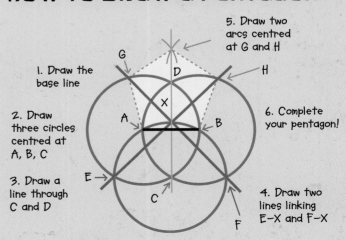

5. Draw two arcs centred at G and H

1. Draw the base line

2. Draw three circles centred at A, B, C

3. Draw a line through C and D

4. Draw two lines linking E–X and F–X

6. Complete your pentagon!

37

The Inside-out room

Deep inside the MM building, there is a room of mysterious puzzles that need a completely different sort of brain. And guess who's got the most completely different sort of brain in the MM Organization?

At the end of the corridor you'll see a green door just before you get to the stairs. You can walk through the door, then once you're inside you can shut it and lock it behind you. In the corner you'll see a rubber table with lots of stretchy things on it, which we'll look at in a minute. The other side of the room has two red doors and opposite them is a storage space for paper and tape and scissors.

The room goes round a corner and up a slope. On the wall you'll see a triangle made from lots of dice. It has a nice normal puzzle for normal brains, but it also has a SECRET puzzle for special brains: **can you see which die is furthest away?**

There's another red door, then the room turns another corner and you'll find yourself at the top of some stairs.

Come down the stairs, and if you don't want to step on the wet paint keep over by the handrail.

At the bottom of the stairs you find yourself standing by the locked green door! **You're outside the room again, but what happened?**

You've just passed through our inside-out room. It's not difficult to see how it's planned, but it leads to marvellous arguments.

HI, IT'S ME! EVEN IF YOU'RE NO GOOD AT SUMS, YOU COULD STILL TURN OUT TO BE A MATHS GENIUS.

WHATEVER YOU DO, DON'T TRY TO COUNT THE SHELVES.

THE OPPOSITE FACES OF A DIE SHOULD ALWAYS ADD UP TO 7. CAN YOU SPOT THE FAKE? THE ANSWER IS ON PAGE 41.

HMM ... THESE STAIRS LOOK A BIT ODD.

After you went into the room, exactly when did you get out? And if you were never inside the room, who locked the door? And if it isn't a room, what is it?

Most of the maths in this room is called **topology** and it helps people work out how space is put together and whether you can do time travel or exist in two places at once. All this might sound a bit fantastic, but it starts with a few simple ideas, so see how you get on. Good luck!

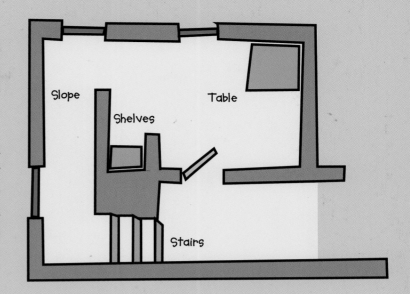

THE IMPOSSIBLE DOORS

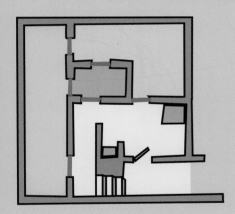

The three red doors lead to other rooms which are all linked by more red doors. Can you find a way to walk through all six red doors, but only passing through each door once?

If you can get through all six red doors then you've cheated! To find out if this sort of puzzle is possible you need to count how many rooms have an odd number of red doors. If it's more than two, the puzzle is impossible! Here all four rooms have three doors, so you can't do it.

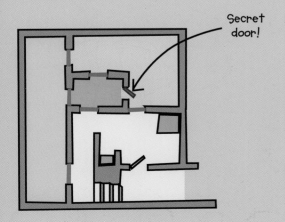

Secret door!

Now two of the rooms have four doors, and four is an even number. This only leaves two rooms with an odd number of doors, so the puzzle should be possible. Can you find a way using all the red doors and the blue door only one time each?

You'll need to start in a room with odd doors, and finish in the other room with odd doors!

HOW TO CUT THINGS UP AND LEAVE THEM IN ONE PIECE

> IF YOU CUT SOMETHING DOWN THE MIDDLE YOU GET TWO BITS, YES? WELL NO, NOT ALWAYS...

Get a strip of paper and tape the ends together to make a band. Draw a line along the middle of one side all the way round until it joins up. If you cut it along the middle you get two pieces. Easy!

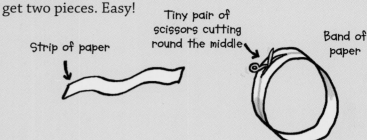

Strip of paper

Tiny pair of scissors cutting round the middle

Band of paper

Extra twist

Now get another strip of paper, but give one end a half twist before you tape the ends together. (This sort of loop is called a **mobius strip**.) Now cut the paper all the way along the middle. When you finish you only get one piece! Thag our Mathemagician likes to perform this as a magic trick if he can find an audience.

> WELCOME TO CELEBRITIES AT THE DENTIST!

> WATCH THIS!

> WHERE DID HE COME FROM?

> I'LL CUT THIS IN HALF ALL THE WAY ROUND...

SNIT SNIT

> DAH-DAH!

> AARGHHH!

> OOH! THAT WAS GOOD!

A mobius strip has a very special use. If you try to colour in one side all the way round and leave the other side blank, you can't! This is because it only has one side. This makes the mobius strip very useful for fan belts, which connect two wheels going round. If ever you see a big old traction engine with a fan belt, you'll see there is a twist in it. This is because a normal fan belt would quickly wear down on the side that touches the wheels. A mobius fan belt lasts twice as long!

Have you got a special maths superbrain?

If you stare at a mobius strip for long enough it isn't too hard to see what's going on, so now we're going to really test your brain. First you need to cut a cross out of a sheet of paper.

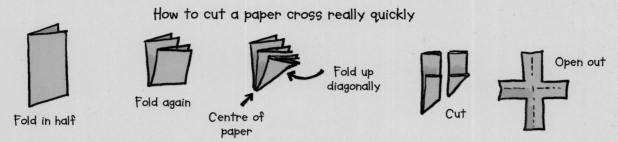

How to cut a paper cross really quickly

Fold in half

Fold again

Centre of paper

Fold up diagonally

Cut

Open out

When you've made your cross, stick the opposite legs together to make two plain loops.

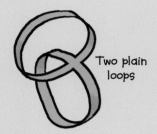

Two plain loops

The big question is – if you cut round the middle of both loops, how many separate bits will you end up with?

IS IT FOUR? TWO? JUST ONE? 743½?

Some people can see the answer immediately! The rest of us need to cut along the middle of both loops and see how many bits we get. The result is so good you might want to put a rectangular frame around it. (Gosh! Where would you suddenly get a rectangular frame from? You won't know the answer until you try this.)

There's one more test to see if you're a maths superbrain...

Make another cross and then stick the opposite legs to make two loops, but this time put a half twist in one loop so it becomes a mobius strip. Before you cut round the middle of both loops, ask yourself:

• How many bits will you get?

• What will they look like?

Is it obvious to you? Really? No cheating? That's awesome.

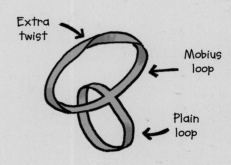

Extra twist

Mobius loop

Plain loop

FAKE DIE ANSWER:

THE FAKE DIE ... IS THE ONE AT THE BOTTOM RIGHT CORNER SHOWING 5 AND 2. IF THE OPPOSITE SIDES ARE SUPPOSED TO ADD UP TO 7 THEN THE 5 CANNOT BE NEXT TO THE 2!

By now you'll know if you've got a maths superbrain, and if you have then you're the kind of person who could unlock the secrets of the universe. What's more, you might even understand the next bit...

when do Broken spectacles = knickers?

Now that your brain has warmed up, let's see what's on the rubber table! Everything on it is made of super-stretchy rubber so the good thing is that measurements and size don't matter. The only things that are important are HOLES. You are not allowed to make any holes and you are not allowed to take any away.

If holes are the only things that matter, which of these objects do you think is most like the mug?

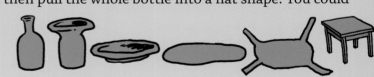

The answer is the CD, because it has one hole in it. The mug also has one hole for the handle. You could thread them both onto a bit of string and hang them up if you wanted to.

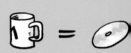

Did you think the bottle was more like the mug? It isn't, because the bottle only has an opening at the top. (It's not a hole because you couldn't thread it onto a bit of string.) If the bottle was made of runny rubber you could stretch the opening right out and then pull the whole bottle into a flat shape. You could then stretch some bits out to make legs and turn it into a table, but you can't make it into the mug or the CD.

The only thing we care about is that we didn't need to make or mend any holes. Therefore: bottle = table.
Don't you wish all sums were like this?

The knickers and the professor's broken spectacles both have two holes, and so some people would have trouble telling which is which!

Creepy curves

There's a great celebration going on in the Murderous Maths research lab at the moment. They must have done something amazing but what could it be? Have they discovered a new number that smells of chocolate? Have they found a square with five corners? Or even more unlikely – has one of them tucked his shirt in?

IT'S OUR NEW INVENTION!

WHOOPY-DOO!

How very brilliant. It's a glass cone that's nearly full of water with a thin film of blue oil floating on the top. When you move it about the blue oil gives you a set of curved shapes called the conic sections. If you stand it upright and look down from the top you get a circle. **Circles are very important curves in maths because that's the shape of pizzas.**

KIPPER AND TOOTHPASTE! YUM!

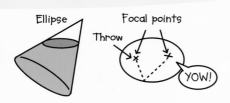

If you tip the cone you get an ellipse. Ellipses are like circles but with two centres called the focal points or 'foci'. If you have an elliptical room and you and a friend stand on the focal points, you can throw a ball in any direction and it'll bounce off the wall and hit your friend on the nose. Ho ho, what fun.

PLANETS GO ROUND THE SUN IN AN ELLIPTICAL ORBIT. ➡ 91

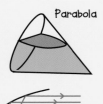

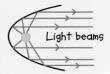

When you lie the cone on its side you get a parabola. This is the shape for the mirrors in spotlights or car headlamps because if you put a light bulb in the focal point, all the light gets sent off in the same direction.

I SAY I SAY – WHY DID FIVE EAT SIX?

BECAUSE SEVEN EIGHT NINE!

BOO! GERROFF!

HAR HAR! NEVER MIND ALL THAT LOT. IF YOU WANT CURVES TAKE A LOOK AT THIS!

YUK!

Oh yuk! It's Professor Fiendish with his pet bottigrubs. These really are revolting beasts which have a bad habit of trying to sniff each other's ... erm ... well, that's why they call them bottigrubs. They also tend to leave slimy trails behind them. But they are good for demonstrating our next topic. Turn over to find out how...

PURSUIT CURVES

Watch what happens when you start four bottigrubs off from the corners of a square box. Each bottigrub is chasing after the one it can see directly in front of it.

As they move along, the four grubs always keep in a square pattern, and the square gets smaller and turns round as they get closer to the middle. When they finally meet up, they'll have left four spiral tracks behind them.

These creepy curves are equiangular spirals 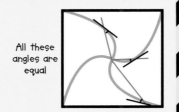57. This means if you draw lines from the middle to anywhere on the curve, the angles they make are always equal.

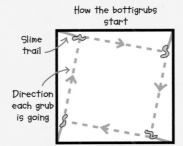

How the bottigrubs start

Slime trail

Direction each grub is going

How the bottigrubs finish

Sniff   Sniff
Sniff   Ahhhh

All these angles are equal

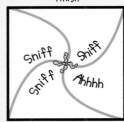

HOT BRAIN ZONE

HOW FAR DOES EACH BOTTIGRUB TRAVEL TO REACH THE MIDDLE?

What a diabolically evil question! But funnily enough it has a lovely easy answer. They each travel exactly the length of one side of the square! Suppose only one bottigrub was moving. He would only have to go along the side of the square to reach his target. However, although his target is moving, the target is always moving at right angles to him. The target never actually moves nearer or further away, and so the target never affects the distance between them. That's why the distance to the centre is the same as if the target wasn't moving at all!

SOMETHING VERY BIG AND EXTREMELY DANGEROUS

What's the fastest way to roll a wheel down a slope? Just a plain straight ramp looks pretty good. As the wheel goes along it gets faster and faster and by the time it reaches the bottom, it'll be going at maximum speed. But surely the wheel would get to the end faster if it speeded up much more quickly to start with? Of course it would, so let's cut away a bit of the ramp.

Now the first part of the track is a quarter of a circle. The wheel drops down really fast and then shoots all the way along the flat bit at maximum speed.

You'd think this would be the fastest way wouldn't you? Oh no. If you're a real daredevil then look at this!

The cycloid

This curve is called a cycloid. It gives the fastest ride from the top to the bottom, even though it actually slopes upwards at the end! It's a bit hard to believe, so our research team are going to build one and test it.

While they get on with it let's find out a bit more. The strangest thing about the cycloid is that if you want to draw one, the secret is in the shape of the wheel itself! This is because you get a cycloid by rolling a circle along a line. You put a mark on the edge of the circle and then trace out where the mark goes.

Roll the circle to draw out the cycloid.

In the old days people got very excited by cycloids and they found they did all sorts of other odd things. For instance, if you turn the curve upside down it makes the strongest shape for a bridge.

The circle takes up exactly 1/3 of the area under the bridge.

The length of the curve is the same as the square around the circle.

45

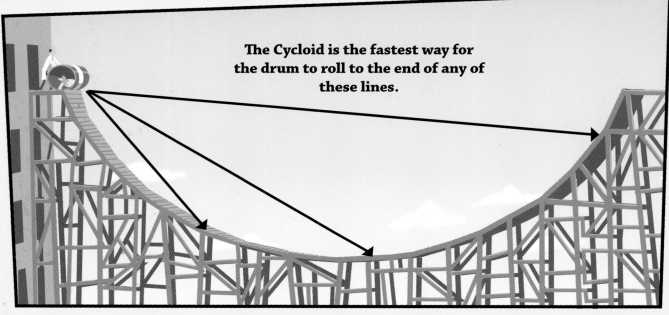

The Cycloid is the fastest way for the drum to roll to the end of any of these lines.

And sure enough, the oil drum will reach any position on the curve in the fastest time possible.

The team have found another oil drum which gives them another experiment to try. They are going to let them go from different heights and see which is first to get to the bottom of the curve.

If both drums are released together they will reach the bottom at the same time!

GET READY ... GO!

YAHOO!

YOW! THAT SOUNDED PAINFUL!

THEY CRASHED EXACTLY IN THE MIDDLE!

KAL-LANGG!

HURRAH!

LOOK!

SERVES HIM RIGHT!

GROAN!

WHICH PART OF A MOVING TRAIN GOES THE WRONG WAY?

Train wheels all have a flange which is a bit that sticks down inside the rail to keep it in place. (Otherwise the train driver would have to steer the train very carefully to keep it on the tracks.) The picture shows that the very edge of the flange draws out a shape called a prolate cycloid. As it goes below the rail it does a little backwards loop!

THE LOWEST PART OF THE WHEEL IS ALWAYS TRAVELLING BACKWARDS!

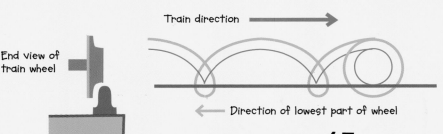

End view of train wheel

Train direction

← Direction of lowest part of wheel

47

the ruler of Golomb

Many thousands of years ago in the Golden Provinces there dwelt the richest man that ever dwelt. His name was the Great Rhun of Jephatti, his wealth was fabulous and his cunning unsurpassed.

One day, in the palace of Jephatti, Thag the Mathemagician was summoned to speak with the Great Rhun.

"My friend, the Ruler of Golomb, has requested your services," said the Great Rhun.

THE RULER REQUIRES YOU TO MAKE HIM ... A RULER.

"A ruler?" repeated Thag. "To measure things?"

"Indeed," said the Great Rhun. "It is to be made from solid gold and must be able to measure one, two or three metres. For the markings he has provided four priceless ancient rubies. If done well you shall be rewarded mightily, but if you fail then you will be fed to the Ghinji."

On hearing his name, the loathsome three-tongued serpent leapt to his master's side and licked his blue lips. Thag hurriedly drew out a design.

"Here's my plan, your fabulousness," said Thag reaching out his hand for the fat red jewels.

The Great Rhun shook his head. "I think not, for I fancy one of these trinkets for myself." So saying, he slipped one of the rubies away into a secret fold buried deep within his gown. "You will make the ruler to measure one, two or three metres, but three marks will need to suffice."

"You ask the impossible!" moaned Thag. The Ghinji grinned and lashed his tail whereupon Thag quickly altered his drawing. "But then the impossible is what I do best. Behold my new plan for the ruler of the Ruler of Golomb!"

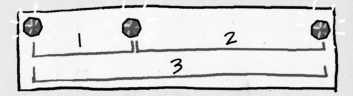

Thag's ruler is a perfect Golomb ruler* because it can measure any number of metres (up to three) and most importantly, there is only one way to do each measurement. That's what makes it a Golomb ruler and not an ordinary one! If your ruler is four metres long you can't make a perfect Golomb ruler with three or even four marks.

Apart from Thag's ruler with three marks, there is only one other perfect Golomb ruler. It has four marks and can measure any distance from one to six metres, but it can't measure any of those distances in more than one way.

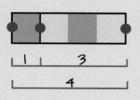

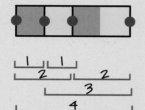

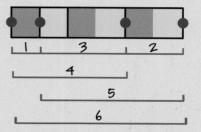

This ruler can't measure 2 metres so it's not perfect

This ruler measures 1 metre and 2 metres in two ways so it's not perfect either

There are no other perfect Golomb rulers that are longer than six metres or use more than four marks!

*These rulers are named after an American maths professor called Solomon W Golomb who probably has the best name in this book.

How Golomb rulers can help to detect aliens

There are lots of bits of maths that just look like silly puzzles to keep maths fans happy, but then they turn out to be really useful. Golomb rulers aren't so good for measuring but they can help us detect the evil Gollarks from the planet Zog.

Suppose we've got four radio telescope dishes in a line scanning the skies. These dishes work in pairs, and they pick up different radio waves depending on how far the two dishes are apart.

If a Gollark sends a radio message home, we don't know which radio waves the Gollarks will use, so we want to pick up as many different waves as we can.

The best way to arrange our dishes is like the four marks on a perfect Golomb ruler. In the same way that the four marks give six different measurements, the four dishes can pick up six different lots of radio waves!

These two dishes are picking up the signal

(Find out how Golomb rulers could make you famous for ever at www.murderousmaths.co.uk)

How to play 4-dimensional noughts and crosses

Did you know that we live in a three-dimensional world? That's because we can move backwards or forwards, left or right or even jump up and down. If you want to know what life would be like in other dimensions, our research lab has got a machine to demonstrate. Our royal guests are just walking past it now, so let's hope they don't do anything silly.

Oh dear, it looks like our visitors have collapsed into a one-dimensional world. They can't get off this line and they can't even move past each other. What's more, all they can see is along the line which would be like looking down a very long narrow pipe. They have no idea they are being watched by our two-dimensional lab assistants, Shady and Smudge.

Shady can walk around the Queen and King if he wants. He can also see everything in the 1-D world at the same time but he can't see Smudge, because there's a line in the way.

A 2-D world is like a shadow. You can measure how long it is or how wide it is, but it doesn't have any thickness. (A piece of paper might seem 2-D, but it also has a tiny bit of thickness, so if you stack lots of pieces up you can make a pile. You can't make a big pile of shadows because they have no thickness at all.)

We live in a three-dimensional world which means we can see the whole of the 2-D world at the same time. Even though Shady and Smudge have put on some rather groovy trousers, we can see them naked! We can even see their insides and what they had for breakfast. (Smudge had sausages, Shady had toast.) Of course Shady doesn't know that anybody is looking at his insides because he can only see what is in his 2-D world. He can't look out of the page at us.

Here comes the scary bit. Suppose there are some fourth-dimensional people? They will be able to see the whole of our three-dimensional world at once and that means they can see YOU stark naked right now reading this book. They can even see what you had for breakfast. **Yuk!**

THE 4-DIMENSIONAL NOUGHTS AND CROSSES GAME

Some people are so clever they can imagine worlds with lots of extra dimensions. This leads to a rather weird maths joke...

HOW DO YOU IMAGINE A WORLD WITH 8 DIMENSIONS?

IT'S SIMPLE! YOU JU IMAGINE A WORLD N DIMENSIONS...

...THEN LET HO HO

Don't worry if you don't think that's funny, you have to have a special maths brain for it. Instead we're just going to have a nice little game of noughts and crosses (which some people call Tic Tac Toe). Two people take turns to put X and O in the boxes, and the first person to make a line of three wins.

First of all we'll bring back our royal visitors and let them play the game in 1-D. All they need are three boxes in a line, but unfortunately there is a slight problem with the 1-D version...

NO ONE CAN W

Now we'll play the norm 2-D version which has thr boxes going across and thr going down. Off we go...

THIS IS BETTER.

BUT THE PERSON WHO STARTS NEARLY ALWAYS WINS!

In ancient times people had a better w playing noughts and crosses. They m out a grid, then had three counters each. took turns to put their counters on squ and then took turns to move a counter u one person had a line. A counter can onl moved on to an empty square next to it, a it can't be moved diagonally.

Moving on to the 3-D version, we have three boxes going across, three going down and three coming out at you! The rules are slightly different. Here the players take turns until all the boxes are filled up, then the person with the most straight lines wins.

We've marked in some winning lines to show the possibilities.

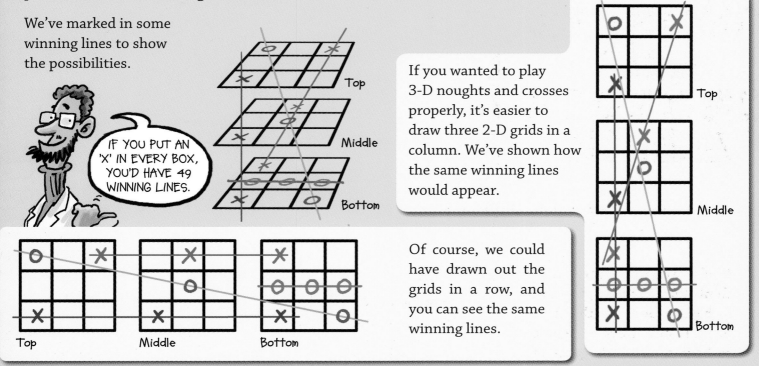

IF YOU PUT AN 'X' IN EVERY BOX, YOU'D HAVE 49 WINNING LINES.

Top

Middle

Bottom

If you wanted to play 3-D noughts and crosses properly, it's easier to draw three 2-D grids in a column. We've shown how the same winning lines would appear.

Top

Middle

Bottom

Top   Middle   Bottom

Of course, we could have drawn out the grids in a row, and you can see the same winning lines.

Here's the good bit. If we draw the grids out in both directions we move into the fourth dimension! Now there are hundreds of ways you can draw a straight line of three.

Each winning line either has to be on one grid (like a normal 2-D game) or across three grids.

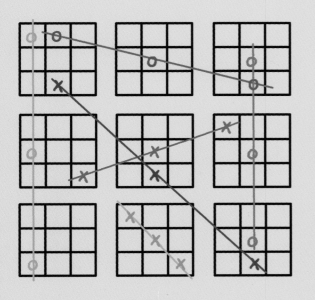

When you see a line going across three grids, imagine the grids are stacked up like the 3-D version and then see if the line would be straight!

So go on, draw a 4-D grid out and then get a friend to play. You might not be able to see what they had for breakfast, but you will be able to see the game in four dimensions.

Shady has to be two-dimensional to see the King and Queen in their one-dimensional world. We have to be three-dimensional to see Shady's 2-D world. But if you can see this game in four dimensions, then while you're playing it, you must be five-dimensional!

How to look perfect

Fashion magazines and TV shows are always trying to tell us how to look perfect, so up in the MM art department, we decided to have a competition.

As you can imagine, a couple of desperate people immediately turned up and tried to impress us.

Unfortunately for Pongo and Veronica, neither of them are quite as gorgeous as our three finalists.

So which one looks the most perfect? Is it the sunflower, the undersea shellfish or an ancient Greek building? It's a very hard decision to make but luckily we've got this thing to help us. It's called the Golden Rectangle. Isn't it gorgeous?

Thousands of years ago people studied rectangles to decide which was the nicest shape to look at. Some were too fat and some were too thin, and gradually they settled on the rectangle where the sides were in the ratio of 1·618 to 1.

This ratio is called the **divine proportion** or the **golden ratio** and it has its own special sign φ which is the Greek letter called 'phi'.

Golden Rectangle

1

1·618

Too fat

Too thin

HOW TO DRAW a GOLDEN RECTANGLE

To be honest φ isn't exactly 1·618. The formula for the absolutely perfect ratio is:

$$\varphi = \frac{1 + \sqrt{5}}{2} = 1{\cdot}6180339887498948482\ldots$$

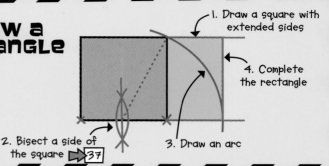

1. Draw a square with extended sides

4. Complete the rectangle

2. Bisect a side of the square ➡ 37

3. Draw an arc

Apart from being gorgeous, this rectangle has a neat trick. If you cut a square off the end, the bit you're left with is another golden rectangle. It might be smaller, but if you divide the long side by the short side you'll get φ again. If you chop a square from this new golden rectangle you'll get another even smaller one.

The number φ does the same trick in its own way. If you put 1 ÷ 1·618 into a calculator you get 0·618.

It's time to bring on our first contestant for the Perfect Figure. All the way from the top of the Acropolis in Athens, will you please welcome the one and only **PARTHENON!**

Square

Another golden rectangle

Square

Another golden rectangle

THAT'S AWESOME.

HUH! IT DOESN'T LOOK VERY PERFECT TO ME. WHEN'S MY TURN?

YOU'LL BE ON AFTER WE'VE MET FIBONACCI.

This fabulous temple was built for the Greek goddess of wisdom, Athena. Even though it's almost 2,500 years old, it's still easy to see how the height, the columns and the roof support are based on golden rectangles. One of the designers was the sculptor Phidias, and phi is named after him.

THE FIBONACCI SERIES

Leonardo Fibonacci was born in Italy in 1175 close to where they were building the not very famous Straight Up Tower of Pisa. Over the next 70 years the tower became the very famous Leaning Tower of Pisa and Leonardo became the greatest mathematician in Europe. One of the best things he did was to get Europe using the excellent Hindu-Arabic 0123456789 number system. If it wasn't for him we might still be doing sums in Roman numerals such as MDCCXXVIII ÷ LIV = XXXII. (That's 1728 ÷ 54 = 32 to you.)

Leonardo was studying the rabbit problem.
(Maybe rabbits were burrowing under the tower and that's why it started to lean over. We don't think it's very likely, but just in case it turns out to be true, remember you read it here first.)

There are several versions of the rabbit problem that all lead to the same answer. In this version we'll start with one pair of rabbits. After one month they produce another pair, after a second month they produce a second pair and then they stop. The new rabbits also produce two pairs in two months. **How many new pairs of rabbits are produced each month?**

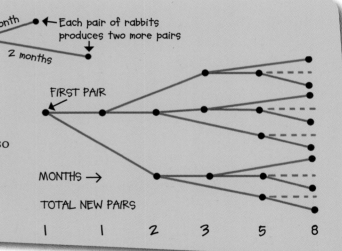

The answers match up with this series of numbers:

0   1   1   2   3   5   8   13   21   34   55   89   144   233   377...

You start with a zero which doesn't do much, so like a lot of the best things in maths you get things going by putting in a ONE. You then add the two numbers together to get 0 + 1 = 1 and write that down as your next number. Then you add the last two numbers 1 + 2 = 3 and then 2 + 3 = 5 and keep going. Further on you'll see that 55 + 89 = 144 and so on.

The fun starts when you pick a number from the series and divide it by the one before. The higher the numbers are, the nearer you get to φ.

Suppose we pick 8 and divide it by 5. We get 1·6. This is quite close to 1·618, but if we pick 34 ÷ 21 we get 1·619. It's even closer!

If you don't like doing sums, there's another way to link the Fibonacci series to the golden rectangle. You draw one little square. On the side of it you draw another little square. You then draw another square to lie alongside the first two, and then another and another. The more squares you add on, the closer your shape gets to a golden rectangle.

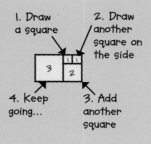

1. Draw a square 2. Draw another square on the side 3. Add another square 4. Keep going...

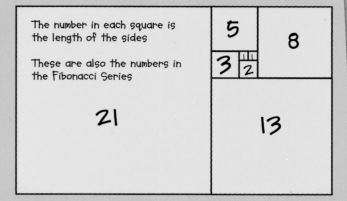

The number in each square is the length of the sides

These are also the numbers in the Fibonacci Series

It's time to see how perfect our second contestant looks. Direct from the bottom of the Indian Ocean, and looking almost exactly as it did millions of years ago, please welcome the **NAUTILUS!**

HI COUSIN!

If you get the set of squares you've just drawn and put a quarter circle in each one you get a super spiral that's almost identical to the shell of the nautilus.

It's the same spiral you get when you see a satellite picture of a cyclone and the clouds are hundreds of miles across!

WHAT'S SO PERFECT ABOUT THAT THING?

THE SHELL SHAPE IS AN EQUIANGULAR SPIRAL!

THAT'S NOTHING, YOU SHOULD SEE A GALAXY SPIRAL! ➤93

Finally it's time to introduce our third contestant...

AT LAST, IT'S MY TURN! ABOUT TIME TOO.

...but before we do, let's have a look at those numbers in that Fibonacci series again.

WHAT

FIVE ODD THINGS ABOUT THE FIBONACCI SERIES:

0-1-1-2-3-5-8-13-21-34-55-89

1. Every third number is EVEN.

2. It can convert miles to kilometres!

MILES	5	8	13	21	34	55
KM	8	13	21	34	55	89

 **3.**

HOT BRAIN ZONE

It makes Pythagorean Triples!  It's amazing how two completely unconnected bits of maths can link up. Who would have thought right-angled triangles were linked to rabbits, eh?

After 5, every second number is the hypotenuse of a right-angled triangle that has whole numbers for the other sides!

$39^2 + 80^2 = 89^2$

89

39

80

1   1   2   3   **5**   8   **13**   21   **34**   55   **89**

The triangle sides: 3,4,5   5,12,13   16,30,34   39,80,89

The middle number always equals the numbers in the last triangle added together! Here, 3 + 4 + 5 = 12

The smallest number always equals the Fibonacci number you missed out minus the smallest number in the last triangle. Here 21 − 5 = 16

This fact is guaranteed to make your maths teacher gasp at your great brain!

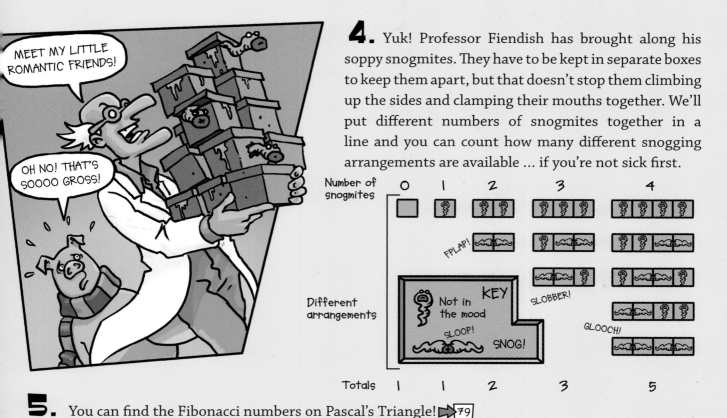

4. Yuk! Professor Fiendish has brought along his soppy snogmites. They have to be kept in separate boxes to keep them apart, but that doesn't stop them climbing up the sides and clamping their mouths together. We'll put different numbers of snogmites together in a line and you can count how many different snogging arrangements are available ... if you're not sick first.

Number of snogmites	0	1	2	3	4
Totals	1	1	2	3	5

5. You can find the Fibonacci numbers on Pascal's Triangle! 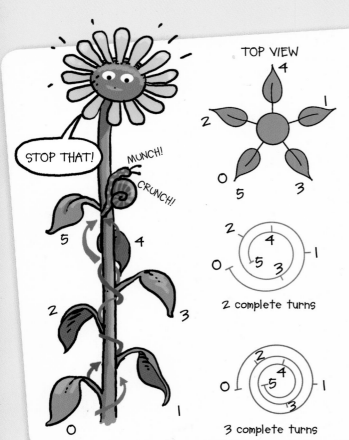 → 79

Right, now let's see why the sunflower is perfect.
Look at how the leaves stick out of the stem.

Call the lowest leaf number zero. Imagine a red snail climbing up the stem winding past each leaf in turn leaving a trail behind it. If you have a sunflower that has been allowed to grow straight up and the pot hasn't been moved since you planted it, then when the snail gets to leaf 5, it'll be directly above leaf zero. You will also find the red slime trail goes round the stem 2 times.

If a blue snail goes up, winding round the other way it will go round the stem 3 times.

2 + 3 = 5 which is one of the sums that makes up the Fibonacci series. This arrangement is a neat way of ensuring the leaves don't end up directly above each other which would block out sunlight.

Almost all plants arrange their leaves or flower petals in some way that links to the Fibonacci series. If you try picking the leaves off a brussels sprout one by one you'll see they grow out of the stem in a regular spiral.

The arrangements of the seeds in the sunflower head also demonstrate Fibonacci spirals. If you look carefully you might see 34 spirals going one way and 55 going the other way.

34 spirals   55 spirals

A Note about Music

There's all sorts of odd noises coming from the MM canteen at the moment. The people from Fogsworth Manor have offered to delight us with a concert tonight and Binkie Smallbrains has ordered a 'Build Your Own Organ' kit, which comes complete with keyboard and pipes.

At this point we'll take a look at Binkie's keyboard to see what's going on.

A keyboard is divided into groups of notes called octaves. The two 'C' notes here are an octave apart. If you start at the low C and move up the notes playing them one at a time including the black ones, these are all the semitones and each note sounds higher than the one before. (If you play this on a real keyboard it sounds like a bit of exciting film music. Ooh-er!) When you've moved up 12 semitones, you've reached the top of the octave.

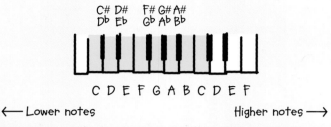

← Lower notes   Higher notes →

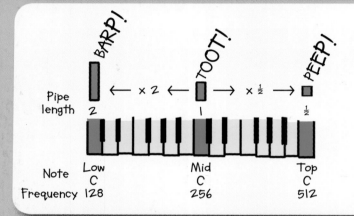

When Binkie pushes a key down, the air in the pipe vibrates and his ears can hear it. The faster the air vibrates, the higher the note sounds.

If the pipe is making the air vibrate 256 times every second, this is called a frequency of 256. This frequency gives you a note of middle C. (Some people say middle C is 262 or 264, but we'll stick with 256 as it makes the sums easier!)

If you cut the pipe in half, the frequency doubles to 512 and you get a note that sounds one octave higher. This is top C and if you play the two notes together they blend perfectly.

If you double the length of the pipe you get low C. To do that we need somebody who can weld pipes together.

If you keep halving or doubling the lengths of the pipes you can get a whole range of C notes going from earth-rumbling subsonic low Cs to screeching little high Cs that could kill bats. But how can Binkie get the other notes?

62

The secret is that if you cut a pipe to $\frac{2}{3}$ length you get a note that's seven semitones higher. If you start with a middle C pipe and keep on chopping it to $\frac{2}{3}$ of the length the sequence of notes goes C-G-D-A-E-B. Then it gets exciting. If you count seven semitones above B you get to the black note just above F which is called F# or F sharp. Then you go on to get C# G# D# A# then F and finally a KILLER C.

Here's how the notes you make would fit on a keyboard.

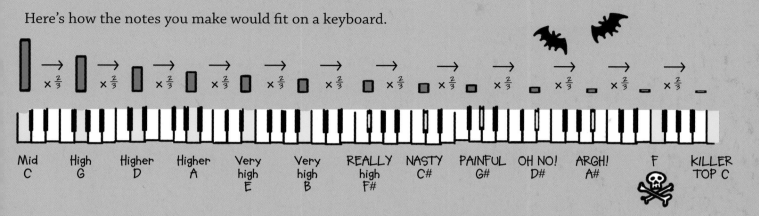

| Mid C | High G | Higher D | Higher A | Very high E | Very high B | REALLY high F# | NASTY C# | PAINFUL G# | OH NO! D# | ARGH! A# | F | KILLER TOP C |

Once you've made these notes you can double up the pipe lengths to fill in the rest of the keyboard, but it'll take ages before you get a decent F note. You need to chop a C pipe by two thirds 11 times to make just one extremely dangerous high F. You'd need to take 64 of these Fs and weld them all together to make the F above middle C.

THERE MUST BE AN EASIER WAY TO GET F!

When we started with our C pipe, we multiplied the length by $\frac{2}{3}$ to move up 7 semitones to get G. But if we divided the length by $\frac{2}{3}$ we'd move down 7 semitones to a very low F!

If you want to divide by a fraction, that's the same as turning the fraction upside down and multiplying. So $\div \frac{2}{3}$ is the same as $\times \frac{3}{2}$. This means we need to get a C pipe and add on half the length and see what we get.

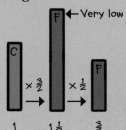

WHAT'S THAT FOR?

IT'S A VERY LOW F.

GOOD SHOW!

Very low F isn't much use, so we'll cut it in half and just get a normal F. You'll see it turns out to be exactly $\frac{3}{4}$ of the length of the C pipe. That's handy!

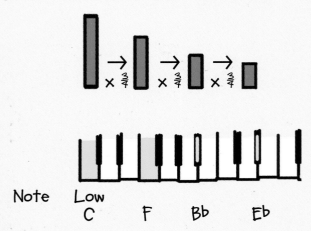

If you cut a pipe to $\frac{3}{4}$ length the note rises five semitones so if you start with your C pipe you can get F and the other notes much faster. After F you get B♭ or B flat which is the black note below B. Then you get E♭, A♭, D♭, G♭ then B, E, A, D, G and finally another KILLER C.

So just by using the simple fractions $\frac{1}{2}$, $\frac{2}{3}$, $\frac{3}{4}$ and then doing a bit of doubling, you can get all the notes in music! Isn't that neat?

WHY YOUR KEYBOARD IS NEVER QUITE IN TUNE

You'll notice when we chopped pipes by $\frac{2}{3}$ we made the sharps, but when we chopped pipes by $\frac{3}{4}$ we made the flats. On a keyboard you use the same black notes to play both the sharps and flats, but they are not exactly the same! Most of the white notes are very slightly wrong too.

Suppose you want to cut your middle C pipe into a very high B. This is 35 semitones above middle C so you've got two choices.

- Chop it into $\frac{2}{3}$rds 5 times. The length will be $\dfrac{2 \times 2 \times 2 \times 2 \times 2}{3 \times 3 \times 3 \times 3 \times 3} = 32/243 = 0{\cdot}1317$.

- Chop it into $\frac{3}{4}$s 7 times. The length will be $\dfrac{3 \times 3 \times 3 \times 3 \times 3 \times 3 \times 3}{4 \times 4 \times 4 \times 4 \times 4 \times 4 \times 4} = 2187/16384 = 0{\cdot}1335$.

The lengths are not the same because the two Bs are different. If you happen to be a brilliant violin player and you know which B you want, you can get it by putting your fingers in a slightly different position on the strings. All you can do on a keyboard is bang the notes in front of you, sing loudly and hope for the best.

The Department of Random Thinking

Mind where you step, it's a bit strange in here. This is where we come to think up wild new ideas, and then we work out if they are right or wrong. New ideas are called theorems and later on we've got a very special one to show you. It doesn't involve any numbers or measuring, and yet if you can work it out you'll be famous for ever!

Theorems can be about anything, so try this one for starters...

THE POTATO CRISP THEOREM

It is always possible to cut two crisps that are exactly the same shape, from two different-shaped potatoes.

It doesn't matter what shapes your two potatoes are, and what's more, there are an infinite number of ways to do it. We can prove it to you too, but be warned. Some people find this a bit scary because we're going to use GHOST potatoes.

Imagine you have two ghost potatoes that can pass through each other. Push them together so that they overlap.

Draw around where the two different skins meet – and there's your crisp!

The crisp that you can cut from both potatoes!

Line goes round where the skins meet

THE PANCAKE THEOREM

If you put two pancakes of any shape and size on a table, there is always a way to chop them both exactly in half with one straight cut.

Wahey! This is just the sort of thing we like to test, so we'll get Pongo McWhiffy to help us. His pancakes look lovely and shiny and brown. They also happen to be waterproof thanks to his special extra ingredient.

I ADD VARNISH!

Even though Pongo's pancakes taste like biting the end off a skateboard, they're perfect for us because they don't bend. This is vital because we're going to ask Pongo to balance his pancakes on the end of a straw.

Centre of gravity

When Pongo has found the balance point, he marks it with a little X. This is called the **centre of gravity**.

Now Pongo puts two pancakes on the table and cuts along a straight line through both centres of gravity. The two halves on one side of the line will weigh exactly the same as the other two halves.

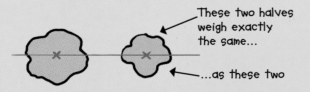

These two halves weigh exactly the same...

...as these two

You have to admire Arthur Stone and John Tukey who came up with this great theorem, especially when you see what they did next.

THE HAM SANDWICH THEOREM

There's no excuse for not dividing a ham sandwich absolutely fairly.

The pancake theorem deals with two flat shapes, but when we move into three dimensions, we can also cut three things exactly in half with one cut.

To test this we need two bits of bread (any size or shape) and a slice of ham in the middle. The theorem doesn't say what the vegetarian options are, but we advise against trying this with honey.

Each of the three bits has a centre of gravity somewhere in the middle and you can easily find this with a piece of cotton and a high-powered laser beam. **FFFZAPPP!**

How to find the centre of gravity of any lumpy thing using a piece of cotton and a laser beam

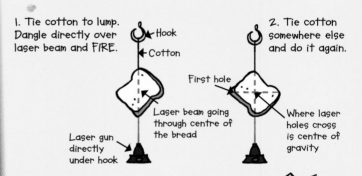

1. Tie cotton to lump. Dangle directly over laser beam and FIRE.

Hook

Cotton

Laser beam going through centre of the bread

Laser gun directly under hook

2. Tie cotton somewhere else and do it again.

First hole

Where laser holes cross is centre of gravity

It doesn't matter how you arrange your sandwich. When you make your cut you just need to be sure it goes through all three centres of gravity, then each of the pieces will be divided exactly into two. Your cut might need to be slanted over rather than vertical, but it is possible.

Arthur and John went on to say that in four dimensions you can divide four things exactly, and in five dimensions you can divide five things and so on, but sadly we haven't invented five-dimensional sandwiches yet so we can't test it.

WHY ON EARTH IS THERE ALWAYS A CYCLONE BLOWING SOMEWHERE?

One of the strangest theorems has to be the **fixed point theorem**. If you're clever enough you can explain it with long numbers, funny letters and signs that look like dead insects, but most normal people wouldn't have a clue what you mean. However, we can see some of the odd things this theorem does. Try this:

- Draw out two identical grids of numbers, one on paper and one on clear polythene.

- Crumple up the polythene and drop it on the paper grid.

- There will always be one number on the polythene directly above its matching number on the paper.

It's one of those things that you think can't be true but it JUST IS.
The fixed point theorem comes up everywhere, even outside Pongo's burger bar.

FANCY A PANCAKE, VERONICA?

YUK!

One morning the terribly lovely Veronica Gumfloss leaves Pongo's at 10:00 and walks right up Gas Street. She stops several times to chat to boys and slap on extra lipstick. She finally reaches the chocolate-fountain booth at exactly 11:00. The next day she does the opposite journey. She leaves the chocolate fountain at 10:00 and walks down Gas Street stopping to chat to her lipstick and slap boys then reaches Pongo's at 11:00.

Here's the weird bit. There has to be one place along the street that she passes at exactly the same time on both days! It sounds very unlikely, but it's true. Suppose there were two Veronicas and she did both walks at the same time on the same day. It doesn't matter how much lipstick or boys are involved, at some point the two Veronicas have to cross. That's when and where the same time and place happened!

The strangest thing that the fixed point theorem does is explain why there always has to be a cyclone blowing somewhere on the Earth. (A cyclone is like a tornado or whirlwind. It has a thin blast of wind in the middle going straight upwards and the air rushing in to fill the gap blows around in a circle. It's a bit like the water going down a plughole.)

How a bit of air moves in a cyclone

What happens if you try to comb all the hair flat

Imagine you've got a football covered in spiky hair. If you try to comb all the hair flat you can't do it. There always has to be at least one bit sticking up. (This is the 'fixed point' of the fixed point theorem.) Now imagine that the football is the Earth and each hair is an arrow showing which way the wind is blowing. The sticking up hair represents the wind going straight upwards – and that's the centre of the cyclone!

HOW TO DRAW YOUR WAY TO EVERLASTING FAME!

The idea is that you draw a map with lots of different countries which can be any size or shape you like. You then have to colour the map in so that no two countries with the same colour share the same border.

 This little map obeys the rules, because the red and green countries are only touching at a corner.

For this map we've had to use an extra colour because the red and grey countries share a border.

  These two little maps both need four colours to obey the rules.

Here's the tricky part. The **four-colour map theorem** says that you will never need more than four different colours. It doesn't matter how complicated your map is!

When you colour your map in you have to make sure you don't go wrong. You'd need a fifth colour to fill in the areas marked '?' on this map.

 However if the colours had been planned correctly, then it would have been possible to fill in all the countries just using four colours.

The good bit is that nobody is absolutely certain that you never need more than four colours for any map, so here's how you could be famous for ever.

EITHER: you have to design a map that needs at least five colours!

OR: you have to prove that you only need four colours. This is likely to be tricky. In 1976 there was a computer program that supposedly proved it, but the answer was so complicated that nobody understood it. It's a lovely simple problem, so the maths world is waiting for a lovely simple answer! It'll take a bit of real sideways thinking but if you manage it, you'll get coffee-stained fan mail and you'll be invited to give lectures all over the world to lovely mad people with random hair and odd socks.

YOU JUST NEED THREE GHOST POTATOES AND A HAM SANDWICH...

The four-colour map theorem doesn't apply to real maps because although nobody usually minds what colour the countries are, they like the sea and lakes to be blue. As soon as you start saying that two or more areas have to be the same colour then you will probably need more than four colours. Here we need blue for the lake and the sea plus four more colours.

Lake Whiffy

The Brown Sea

THE ONE-LINE DOODLE

If you just draw one continuous line that loops over itself, you'll never need more than three colours.

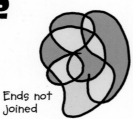
Ends not joined

And if the two ends of the line join together, you'll only need two colours!

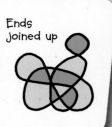
Ends joined up

ESCAPE FROM GRIMSTATE

If you doodle out a great big loop that never crosses itself, then something rather strange can happen, as this case from the police files shows...

City: Grimstate
Place: The County Jail

Date: 15 November 1931
Time: 11:45 a.m.

The seven shady men were sitting round the table in the prison cell. Blade Boccelli tossed the jack of spades on to the pile of cards in the middle and stared across at Weasel.

"Nice play Blade," said One-Finger Jimmy. "Ten dollars says you can't beat him, Weasel!"

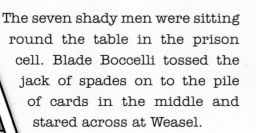
BLADE

WEASEL

ONE FINGER

Half-Smile Gabrianni gave Weasel's shoulder an impatient nudge. "Come on brother, you can't let a Boccelli beat you!" Weasel flexed his knuckles then with a lightning flick of the wrist he slapped the jack of diamonds on to the pile.

"SNAP!" shouted all seven men together. Then "We said it first." then "No you didn't, we did," then "Are you calling us liars?"

Immediately they all leapt to their feet and reached into their jackets for their weapons … but realized they hadn't got any. Feeling a bit silly they all sat down again.

"So what's the score anyway?" Weasel asked the thinnest man.

"They owe us $23,617," said Numbers.

"Yeah, well who cares?" grinned Blade. "As long as we're in here you'll have to whistle for it."

They all laughed. It was rare to see the Boccellis and the Gabriannis laughing together, but the cell was warm and the food was free. Life was a lot easier than being on the outside.

A click of high heels and a cloud of perfume came down the corridor.

"On your feet, boys, it's visiting hours," said Dolly Snowlips. "And I got good news. The governor has agreed that you should get some exercise."

"Exercise?" they all groaned.

"Thanks but no thanks, Dolly," said Blade. "We're just fine in here."

"C'mon you slobs," said a gruff man's voice as the key turned in the lock. "Dolly's only got your good health in mind. I've laid out an exercise area, and running round it will keep you healthy!"

"How can running keep us healthy?"

"Because if you don't run, Nailgun is going to catch you."

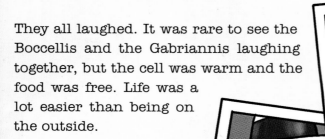

Suddenly a huge growling dog with teeth like vulture's claws bounded into the cell. And equally suddenly, the seven shady men all ran out screaming.

Earlier the governor had been showing Dolly how he'd designed the exercise area.

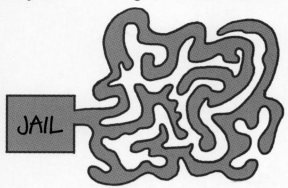

The fence was arranged in one big loop tacked on to the back door of the jail, but when the fence had arrived, it had been longer than he'd expected. This meant he could make the loop a lot more complicated, but it still didn't cross over.

Up in the office the governor was fiddling with a fancy movie-screen machine.

"Would you like to see how they're all getting on, Miss Snowlips?" he asked.

He flicked a switch, and a picture showing part of the exercise area appeared.

"It's an overhead plan. It only shows the middle section, but at least we can see where Nailgun and all the boys are," he explained.

Key: B=Blade P=Porky J=One-Finger Jimmy
H=Half-Smile C=Chainsaw Charlie N=Numbers W=Weasel

Dolly stared at the picture then grinned. "I hate to tell you this, governor, but you've got a hole in that fence somewhere. If your dog is still on the inside then three of the boys are on the outside!"

HOW DID DOLLY KNOW?

If you look at the coloured area on the governor's first little drawing you'll see that one side of the fence is always on the inside, and the other is on the outside. If you start on the inside and cross the fence an odd number of times, you'll end up on the outside. If you cross the fence an even number of times you'll end up back inside. Start at the dog and count how many times you need to cross the fence to reach each person. **Can you see which three have escaped?**

How to win a load of money

If you're tossing coins, throwing dice or dealing cards, here's something amazing to help you win. Just like a lot of the best things in maths it starts with a load of 1s!

Put a row of 1s down each side of a triangle.

Fill in the gaps starting at the top. Each number is made by adding the two numbers above it.

This triangle only has 10 rows, but they can go on for ever, as you'll soon find out!

This thing is usually called **Pascal's Triangle** after the French genius Blaise Pascal who died in 1662, but in Italy they call it Tartaglia's Triangle after the algebra wizard who drew it out 100 years earlier. BUT 300 years before that Yang Hui drew it in China, and before that it had appeared in India and Iran and probably some other places too. We get tons of emotional messages about this, so maybe we should call it 'Nearly Everybody's Triangle'.

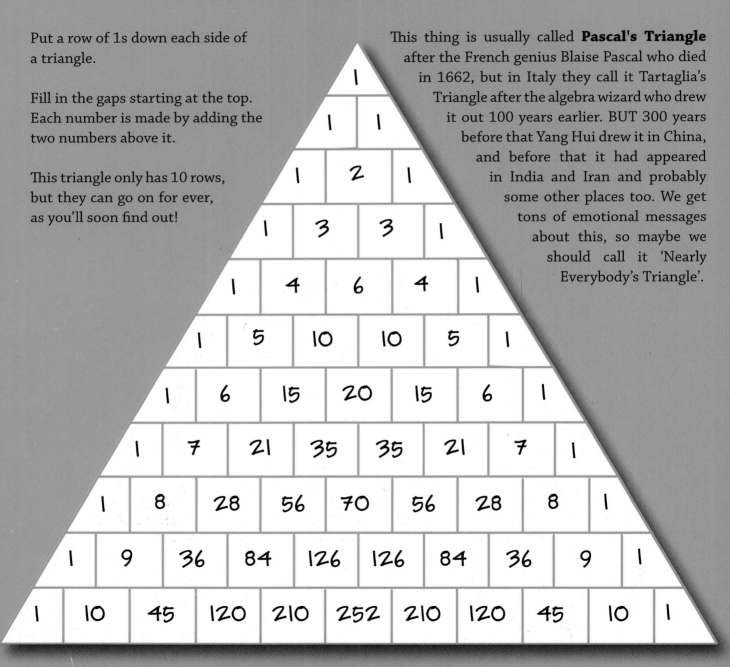

Right then, let's not waste time. Let's join Riverboat Lil who's waiting in the Last Chance Saloon to show us what this thing can do. All she needs is a volunteer...

Heads I Win, Tails You Lose

The first thing to realize here is that three coins can fall in EIGHT different ways! It becomes more obvious if you imagine the pennies are different colours.

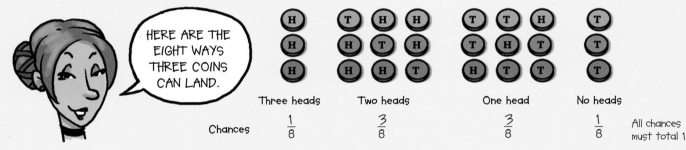

Look at the row of fractions showing the chances ... and now look at the third row of Pascal's Triangle! (That's the one with the 3s in it. We don't count the 1 at the top as a row.)

| Numbers on 3rd row | $\frac{1}{8}$ | $\frac{3}{8}$ | $\frac{3}{8}$ | $\frac{1}{8}$ |

Out of the eight ways the coins can land, only one has three heads, and only one has three tails. This means that on average if Brett plays eight times...

Brett will win TWICE and Lil gives him 2 × $2 = $4
Brett will lose SIX times and he gives Lil 6 × $1 = $6

Therefore Lil can expect to make $2 profit for every eight throws!

Pascal's Triangle can show you what happens when you toss ANY number of coins. Suppose you have NINE coins. Look along the ninth row and you'll see the numbers 1-9-36-84-126-126-84-36-9-1. These are the number of ways you can get nine heads, eight heads, seven heads... and so on! The number 1 on the end of the row is the number of ways you can get no heads – in other words there is just one way of getting all nine tails.

SO CAN IT TELL ME MY CHANCES OF THROWING AT LEAST SEVEN HEADS WITH 9 COINS?

It sure can, Brett. We add up the chances for nine, eight and seven heads – which are 1 + 9 + 36 = 46. We divide this by the total number of chances, 512 (which is all the numbers on the row added up). So it's $\frac{46}{512}$ which is 0·0898 or about 9% 81.

a DODGY DeaL

So what are Brett's chances of picking the three red cards?

To work it out we need to know how many different sets of three cards Brett could pick from the five cards Lil offers him. Our nice Mr Davis has drawn them all out here for us:

This is the only set of three red cards, so the chance is 1/10

You'll see there are 10 different sets, and only one of them has the three red cards. The chance of Brett picking the three red cards is only 1/10 which is 10%.

As Lil has five cards, we look at row 5 of Pascal's Triangle ➡️72.

The number 1 at the beginning tells you how many ways Brett could pick NO cards. If Brett picks one card, there are five different 'sets' because his card could be the ace or 2 or 3 or 4 or 5. If you skip along to the sets of three cards, you'll see it says there are 10 which is what we already worked out!

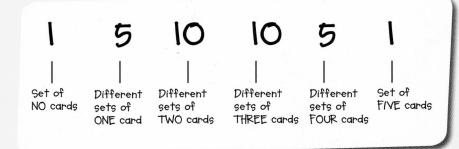

1	5	10	10	5	1
Set of NO cards	Different sets of ONE card	Different sets of TWO cards	Different sets of THREE cards	Different sets of FOUR cards	Set of FIVE cards

THE FULL PACK!

> OK! LET'S PLAY WITH ALL 52 CARDS. I'LL DEAL YOU 13 OF THEM, SO WHAT'S THE CHANCE YOU GET ALL THE 13 HEARTS?

> EVEN I'M NOT DUMB ENOUGH TO BET ON THAT, LIL!

When you play cards, you don't usually worry what order you get them in, and Pascal's Triangle doesn't worry about the order either. But when Brett picked three cards from Lil's set of five, what were the chances he'd pick the ace first and then the 2 and finally the 3?

This makes the sums very different.

To start with Lil has five cards, so Brett's chance of picking the ace is $\frac{1}{5}$. Then Lil has four cards so Brett's chance of picking the 2 is $\frac{1}{4}$. Finally Lil has three cards so Brett's chance of picking the 3 is $\frac{1}{3}$. Multiply these together and you'll find his chance of getting ace-2-3 in order is $\frac{1}{60}$.

Chance of getting 3 cards out of 5 in the right order:

$$\frac{1}{5 \times 4 \times 3} = \frac{1}{60}$$

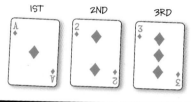

For once Brett is being sensible. To work out the chance we need to know how many different sets of 13 cards you can get from a full pack of 52. We could ask our nice Mr Davis to draw all the possible sets of 13 cards out, but he'd stop being nice very quickly unless we arranged a bit of help for him. We'd need to ask everybody in the whole world to draw out 100 sets of 13 cards each!

A much easier way of working it out is to draw our Pascal's Triangle right down to the fifty-second row, and then count along to find the thirteenth number. This should only take a couple of months, but if you're in a rush there is a formula on the next page to find any number on Pascal's Triangle...

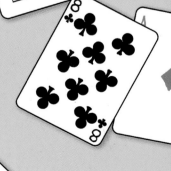

THe FORMULA

The Nth number on the Rth row = $\dfrac{R!}{(R - N)! \times N!}$

We want to know the thirteenth number on the fifty-second row, so N=13 and R = 52.

> HOLD ON TO YOUR HAT, BRETT. HERE COME SOME MIGHTY BIG NUMBERS!

> ! This is the factorial sign. It means you multiply the number by all the other numbers down to 1.
>
> So 4! = 4 × 3 × 2 × 1 = 24. There's a special rule about factorials. 1! = 1 and also 0! = 1.

$$\frac{52!}{(52 - 13)! \times 13!} = \frac{52!}{39! \times 13!} =$$

$\dfrac{52 \times 51 \times 50 \times 49 \times 48 \times 47 \times 46 \times 45 \times 44 \times 43 \times 42 \times 41 \times 40 \times 39 \times 38 \times 37 \times 36 \times 35 \times 34 \times 33 \times 32 \times 31 \times 30 \times 29 \times 28 \times 27 \times 26 \times 25 \times 24 \times 23 \times 22 \times 21 \times 20 \times 19 \times 18 \times 17 \times 16 \times 15 \times 14 \times 13 \times 12 \times 11 \times 10 \times 9 \times 8 \times 7 \times 6 \times 5 \times 4 \times 3 \times 2 \times 1}{39 \times 38 \times 37 \times 36 \times 35 \times 34 \times 33 \times 32 \times 31 \times 30 \times 29 \times 28 \times 27 \times 26 \times 25 \times 24 \times 23 \times 22 \times 21 \times 20 \times 19 \times 18 \times 17 \times 16 \times 15 \times 14 \times 13 \times 12 \times 11 \times 10 \times 9 \times 8 \times 7 \times 6 \times 5 \times 4 \times 3 \times 2 \times 1 \times 13 \times 12 \times 11 \times 10 \times 9 \times 8 \times 7 \times 6 \times 5 \times 4 \times 3 \times 2 \times 1}$

This looks murderous, but don't panic because help is at hand...

It's Thag, our Mathemagician! Stand by for some serious number-crunching.

> ALL THE NUMBERS ON THE BOTTOM CANCEL OUT WITH NUMBERS ON THE TOP AND VANISH! HERE'S ALL THAT'S LEFT!

50 X 49 X 47 X 46 X 43 X 41 X 17 X 4

Thanks Thag! A quick bash on the calculator tells us that the sum comes to 635,013,559,600. This is the thirteenth number on the fifty-second row!

So now we know there are 635,013,559,600 different ways Lil can deal you 13 cards from a pack of 52. Only ONE of these ways has all thirteen hearts!

> SO THE CHANCES OF YOU GETTING ALL 13 HEARTS IS ABOUT ONE IN 635 BILLION...

> ...UNLESS OF COURSE YOU'VE BEEN DOING SOME OF YOUR FANCY DEALING.

DICE AND VULTURE-SPIT COCKTAILS

When Brett was picking cards from Lil, he knew each card would be different. (For instance he couldn't have picked two aces of diamonds.) But when Lil throws some dice, two or more of them might have the same number. This really messes up the sums!

I'LL THROW TWO SIX-SIDED DICE!

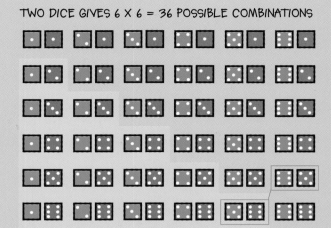

TWO DICE GIVES 6 × 6 = 36 POSSIBLE COMBINATIONS

If both dice are the same colour, these combinations are repeated. Therefore there are only 21 different combinations.

Here's one of the repeated combinations

With two dice there are 6 × 6 = 36 ways they can land, but some of the number combinations are repeated (e.g. 6-5 and 5-6). If you only count repeated combinations once, there are only 21 different number combinations.

This is easy to see with two dice, but what if Lil throws three dice?

Although there are 6 × 6 × 6 = 216 different ways they can land, these ways include six different ways of throwing 1-2-3 as well as three different ways of throwing 1-2-2, and the one and only way of throwing 4-4-4.

SIX ways of throwing any set of three different numbers.

THREE ways of throwing any set with two matching numbers.

ONE way of throwing any set of three matching numbers.

WITH FOUR DICE AND FIVE DICE IT GETS EVEN MORE CONFUSIN'!

So how many different number combinations are possible with three, or four or five dice?

How many different number combinations can a set of SIX-SIDED dice give you?

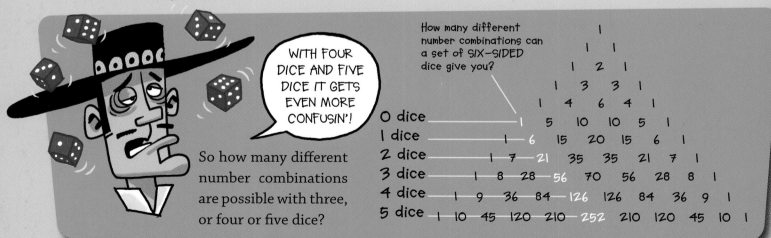

```
                                    1
                                 1     1
                              1     2     1
                           1     3     3     1
                        1     4     6     4     1
0 dice _____ 1     5    10    10     5     1
1 dice _____ 1     6    15    20    15     6     1
2 dice _____ 1     7    21    35    35    21     7     1
3 dice _____ 1     8    28 — 56    70    56    28     8     1
4 dice ____ 1     9    36    84 — 126   126    84    36     9     1
5 dice _ 1    10    45   120   210 — 252   210   120    45    10     1
```

The sums here get really fiddly, but the Murderous Maths research lab found the answer on Pascal's Triangle!

You'll see that even though there are 216 different ways three dice can land, there are only 56 different number combinations.

78

Brett has a choice of four different flavours and he can choose seven times. This is like throwing seven four-sided dice (imagine each dice has the four flavours written on the sides!). We look down the '4' diagonal and then count along to the seventh place. The first '1' above the 4 counts as zero. We get:

NUMBER BRETT CAN PICK: 0 1 2 3 4 5 6 7
DIFFERENT COMBINATIONS: 1–4–10–20–35–56–84–120

Brett has 120 different cocktails he could make!

OT BRAIN ZONE

Some odd things that turn up on Pascal's Triangle!

Add numbers on shallow diagonals to get FIBONACCI SERIES

Normal numbers 1, 2, 3, 4

Triangle numbers 1, 3, 6, 10

Co-efficients of $(a+b)^n$
e.g $(a+b)^4 =$
$a^4 + 4a^3b + 6a^2b^2 + 4ab^3 + b^4$

Add numbers in a row to get powers of 2
e.g $2^5 = 1 + 5 + 10 + 10 + 5 + 1 = 32$

COOL CHAOS!

Finally, here's one of the cutest things about Pascal's Triangle and it doesn't involve any nasty sums. You need to draw out a MASSIVE Pascal's Triangle, and then colour in all the odd numbers.

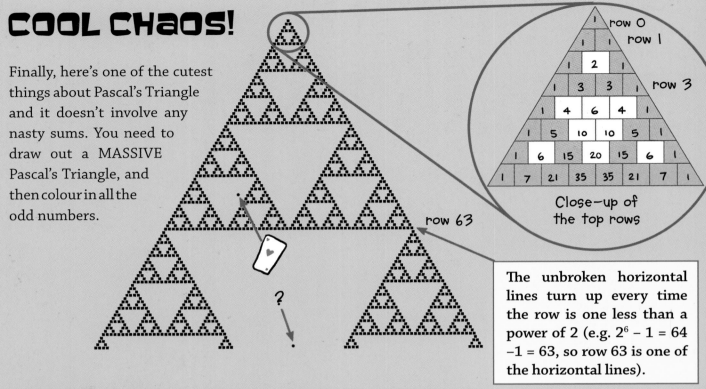

row 63

Close-up of the top rows

The unbroken horizontal lines turn up every time the row is one less than a power of 2 (e.g. $2^6 - 1 = 64 - 1 = 63$, so row 63 is one of the horizontal lines).

Interesting things to know about this pattern:

▶ This Pascal Triangle has 100 rows.

▶ You can make this pattern starting with a plain equilateral triangle. Put a tiny dot anywhere you like inside it. Draw a second dot exactly halfway between the first dot and any corner. Draw a third dot exactly halfway between the second dot and any corner. Keep going drawing more dots. It doesn't matter how you pick the corners, after a few thousand times your dots start to form the pattern of triangles inside triangles inside triangles! This is called **Sierpinski's Triangle** and because you can start anywhere and choose any corner at any time this is a bit of super cool random **Chaos Maths**!

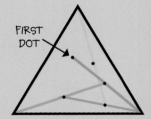

FIRST DOT

The first five dots of a Sierpinski Triangle

▶ The number marked with the ace of hearts is the 13th number on the 52nd row – which tells us Brett's chances of getting all 13 hearts! ➡ 76

▶ There's a good reason why we didn't write all the numbers in. The number marked '?' in the very middle of the hundreth row is 100,891,344,545,564,193,334,812,497,256.

MERCY ME, THAT'S ONE MIGHTY MURDEROUS NUMBER, LIL.

AND IT ALL COME FROM JUST ADDING A FEW LITTLE ONE TOGETHER, BRETT

Riverboat Lil's guide to games

IF YOU LIKE PLAYING GAMES, IT HELPS TO KNOW YOUR CHANCES OF WINNING!

I SAID TURN LEFT! ARGHHH!

What are the chances of things happening?

DEFINITE!	100%	You're reading this book right now
	89%	In a room of 40 people at least two of them share a birthday
ALMOST CERTAIN	83%	You score 9 or less when throwing two dice
	75%	When you get dressed quickly in the dark you put your pants on inside out and/or back to front
HOPEFUL	70%	A spaceship being flown by aliens who can't steer hits the sea instead of coming down on dry land
	62%	You score 10 or more when throwing three dice
50/50 EVENS	50%	You toss two coins and get one head and one tail
	42%	You get a pair when someone deals you five cards
UNLIKELY	33%	The first two aces in a shuffled pack are the same colour
	31%	You get three heads and three tails when tossing six coins
	23%	You get two pairs when you throw five dice
YOU'LL BE LUCKY	11%	You're left-handed
	0%	You feel fine after eating Pongo McWhiffy's curried octopus burger
NO WAY!		

We've already seen how Pascal's triangle shows the patterns and combinations you get with dice and cards. Now we'll look at the exact chances of getting what you need to win games. We usually describe chance with percentages. 100% means something will definitely happen and 0% means something cannot happen.

You can also use fractions like this: What's the chance your granny was born on a Monday or a Tuesday? There are seven days in a week, so the chance of it being one of these two days is 2 out of 7 which makes a fraction of $\frac{2}{7}$.

You can convert any fraction into a percentage by dividing by the bottom number and then multiplying by 100. To convert $\frac{2}{7}$ we do $2 \div 7 \times 100 = 28 \cdot 57\%$.

DICE GAMES

If you throw one dice, there's an equal chance of getting any of the numbers between 1 and 6. If you throw two dice there are 36 ways they can land 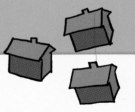[→ 78]. The spots can add up to any number between 2 and 12 but some numbers are far more likely to come up than others. Lil's Wild West version of snakes and ladders has REAL SNAKES. If you add up the chances for the good squares and the chances for the bad squares you can see if it's worth risking! The chances also tell you which square you're most likely to land on.

(The square you're most likely to land on is nasty number 7! But there's only a 16·7% chance this will happen. If you add up all the percentages, you'll find the chances of landing on a good square are about 53% and the chances of landing on a snake square are about 47% so you've got a slightly better chance of getting rich than being bitten by a snake.)

THROW TWO DICE AND SEE WHERE YOU LAND!

When you throw THREE dice the spots can add up to anything between 3 and 18. Here are the different chances:

Total spots	Chance
3 or 18	1/216 = 0·46%
4 or 17	3/216 = 1·39%
5 or 16	6/216 = 2·78%
6 or 15	10/216 = 4·63%
7 or 14	15/216 = 6·94%
8 or 13	21/216 = 9·72%
9 or 12	25/216 = 11·57%
10 or 11	27/216 = 12·5%

MONOPOLY

The chance of throwing three doubles and going to jail is $\left[\frac{1}{6}\right]^3 = \frac{1}{216}$ or 0·46%

Apart from being in jail, Trafalgar Square is the most landed-on square. The three orange squares are the most landed-on set.

For some dice games, you don't add up the spots. Instead, it's more important to see what combinations you get.

In Yahtzee, you throw five dice and you score points for getting combinations such as a full house or straights. You get three throws for each turn. The first time you throw all five dice, then for the next two throws you only have to throw the dice you want to change. This makes it much easier to get different combinations but much harder to work the sums out!

If you could only throw once, your chance of getting a 'Yahtzee', which is all 5 dice the same, is just 0·077%. As you're allowed the two extra throws the chance is 4·6%. This means that for about every 22 turns you have at Yahtzee, you're only likely to get all five dice the same only once.

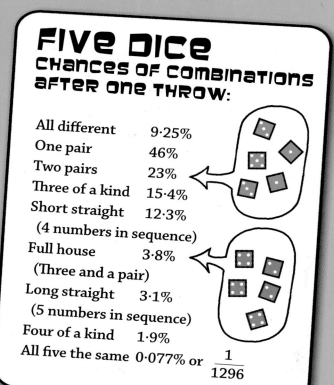

FIVE DICE
CHANCES OF COMBINATIONS AFTER ONE THROW:

All different	9·25%
One pair	46%
Two pairs	23%
Three of a kind	15·4%
Short straight	12·3%
(4 numbers in sequence)	
Full house	3·8%
(Three and a pair)	
Long straight	3·1%
(5 numbers in sequence)	
Four of a kind	1·9%
All five the same	0·077% or $\frac{1}{1296}$

CARD GAMES

There are 52 cards in a normal pack, and they are divided into four different suits of 13 cards each.

In games like whist or bridge you get 13 cards from a pack and it can be a big help if you've got a lot of the same suit. Here are the chances for the number of cards in your longest suit.

> **A VOID suit:** Your chance of an empty suit is about 5%. (In other words all your 13 cards are in three suits and you don't have any of the fourth suit.)

Four-card suit: 35%
Five-card suit: 44%
Six-card suit: 16·5%
Seven-card suit: 3·5%
Eight-card suit: 0·47%
Nine-card suit: 0·037%
Ten-card suit: 0·0017%
Eleven-card suit: 0·000036%
Twelve-card suit: 0·00000032%
Thirteen-card suit: 1 in 159 billion*

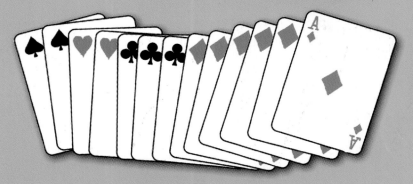

16·5% chance of a six card suit

* This could be any suit. But suppose you hoped to get one particular suit (e.g. all 13 hearts), the chance is $\frac{1}{4}$ of this, which is 1 in 635 billion .

➡ 76

POKER HANDS

If you are dealt five cards, here are the chances of different poker hands:

1 in 650,000: ROYAL FLUSH (A, K, Q, J, 10 all the same suit)

1 in 72,000: STRAIGHT FLUSH (a run of five cards all in the same suit e.g. 7, 8, 9, 10, J all hearts)

1 in 4,000: FOUR OF A KIND

1 in 700: FULL HOUSE (three of a kind AND a pair)

1 in 500: FLUSH (all five cards the same suit)

1 in 255: STRAIGHT (e.g. a run such as 2, 3, 4, 5, 6 but not in the same suit)

2%: THREE OF A KIND (e.g. three aces)

5%: TWO PAIRS (e.g. two eights and two threes)

42%: ONE PAIR (e.g. two queens)

Straight Flush

Full House

> I DREAM OF HOLDIN' A ROYAL FLUSH, LIL!

> KEEP DREAMIN', BRETT. IT'S THE ONLY WAY YOU'RE LIKELY TO GET ONE!

SNAP!

The chance of the top and bottom cards of a pack being a pair is **1 in 17** or **5·88%**

The chance of the first two cards matching is also 1 in 17.

CLUEDO

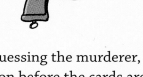

The chance of guessing the murderer, room and weapon before the cards are dealt out: $\frac{1}{9 \times 6 \times 6} = \frac{1}{324}$ or 0·3%.

RIFFLE SHUFFLE

In a perfect **riffle shuffle** you split a pack of 52 cards exactly in half, then sandwich the two halves together alternately. The top card will still be on top and the bottom card stays on the bottom. If you keep going, the pack will return to the starting order after eight shuffles!

The curious chess cupboard

Just along from the games room, our royal visitors have discovered a strange secret!

A normal chessboard has eight squares along each side, so that makes 64 little squares altogether.

When we started our tour we saw how putting a few pennies on a board can build up to a truly murderous number ▶ 7 . Here are a few more of the strange things we know about chessboards!

The Knight's Move

In a game of chess the knight moves about in a strange way. It goes two steps forwards and one to the side. Unless it's near the edge, there are eight squares it can move to, and it always ends up on a different-coloured square to the one it starts on.

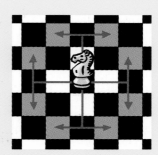

These are the eight squares this knight can jump to.

Naturally lots of people have spent many long hours, days and even weeks trying to see if they can take a knight round every square of the board and get back to the the starting square in exactly 64 moves! There are lots of ways to do it, but our favourite is this one.

The moves are numbered from 1–64 but what makes this really special is that this solution is also a MAGIC SQUARE!

All the numbers in each row add up to 260, and the numbers in each column also add up to 260.

It must have taken somebody months to work this out, but if you think this was a silly waste of time, then we can show you something even sillier!

50	11	24	63	14	37	26	35
23	62	51	12	25	34	15	38
10	49	64	21	40	13	36	27
61	22	9	52	33	28	39	16
48	7	60	1	20	41	54	29
59	4	45	8	53	32	17	42
6	47	2	57	44	19	30	55
3	58	5	46	31	56	43	18

THE CURSED KING!

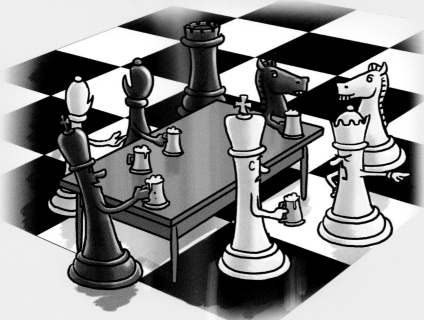

Oh dear, the white king is in trouble! The white queen has caught him partying at the black king's castle. She's making him walk home all the way from the top left square of the chessboard down to the white castle on the bottom right square, and as a special punishment she's put a dreadful curse on him. He's not allowed in until he has walked along *every single possible path* back to the castle!

The king can move one square at a time towards the white castle. He can move down, to the right or diagonally down/right.

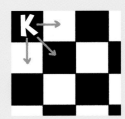

Here are a few of the paths he could take:

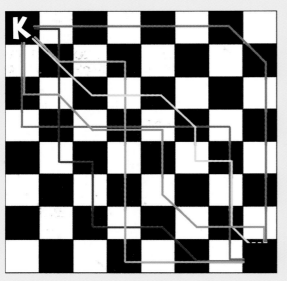

So how many possible paths are there? This is quite a simple little sum but it has a truly murderous answer!

First we'll look at how the king can start out.

There is only one way to reach the square going down, and there is only one way he can get to the square below that. Also there is only one way to reach each of the squares going along the top. However, there are three ways he can reach the first diagonal square. But how many ways can he reach the square marked with a question mark?

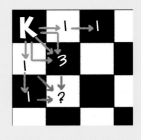

We add up the number of ways from each of the three squares he could come from: 1 + 1 + 3 = 5.

This rule applies to all the squares on the board. For each square, you add up the three numbers above, to the left and diagonally up/left.

For example, you'll see the squares with 25 get it from 7 + 5 + 13 = 25.

K	1	1	1	1
1	3	5	7	9
1	5	13	25	41
1	7	25	63	129
1	9	41	129	321

If the chessboard only had 5 x 5 squares, there would be 321 paths that the king would have to walk.

Have you noticed how the numbers coming down the main diagonal are getting very big very quickly?

Here comes the murderous bit! If you draw out a whole chessboard and write the numbers in, you'll find that the number of paths the king has to walk is ... **48,639!**

THE CHESSBOARD ILLUSION

A spot of space

Up on the roof of the MM building is where we keep our telescopes. We love studying the sky, and it also makes us realize that the Earth is a very nice planet to be on.

- We can breathe the air. (On Venus it's carbon dioxide mixed with sulphuric acid!)

- There is solid ground to walk on. (Jupiter, Saturn, Uranus and Neptune are just giant balls of gas.)

- In most places it's not too hot or cold. (Venus is about 470°C. If you took your oven up to Venus and turned it on full blast, you'd still want to climb inside it to cool down.)

THE EARTH, MOON AND SUN

There's one more thing about Earth that's so obvious, you've probably never thought about it unless you happen to be an evil Gollark invader from the planet Zog.

AT LAST WE'VE ARRIVED! THEIR LOCAL STAR KEEPS THIS PLANET NICE AND BRIGHT AND WARM.

YES, BUT LET'S HAVE A LITTLE NAP FIRST.

STAND BY TO CONQUER AND DESTROY EVERYTHING!

LOOK AT THE STAR!

IT'S GOT A LOT COLDER AND DIMMER!

ARGGHH – THIS PLANET'S SPOOKY!

Our moon appears to be exactly the same size and shape as the sun. That's because although the sun's diameter is 400 times bigger, it happens to be 400 times further away. Earth is the only planet in the solar system which has a moon that does this trick, so aliens wouldn't be expecting it. No wonder they get confused.

Everything in space is so very very tiny that it's impossible to imagine until you make a scale model.

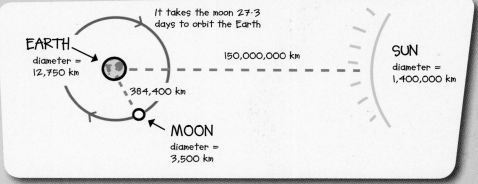

It takes the moon 27·3 days to orbit the Earth

EARTH
diameter = 12,750 km

150,000,000 km

SUN
diameter = 1,400,000 km

384,400 km

MOON
diameter = 3,500 km

HOW TO MAKE A SCALE MODEL OF THE EARTH, MOON AND SUN

1. Paint a medium-sized tree yellow.

2. Go and stand 750 metres (nearly half a mile) away.

3. Hold your arms outstretched with an apple in one hand and a grape in the other.

4. The apple is the Earth, the grape is the moon and the tree is the sun. And just in case anybody thinks you've gone bonkers, tell them you're modelling the terrestial/lunar/solar relationship on a scale of 1:200,000,000. Then they won't think you're bonkers any more. Probably.

HE'S JUST PAINTED THAT TREE YELLOW!

THESE PEOPLE ARE SCARING ME!

HOW TO DRAW A CRESCENT MOON

1. Draw a semi-circle

2. Draw in some horizontal lines

3. Divide the lines in half (or any other fraction you like)

4. Join up the crosses

PLUTO anD CO.

There are nine planets in our solar system if you count Pluto (and *we* do even if some people say it's just a dwarf planet now.) If you're still standing 750 metres from a yellow tree holding a grape and an apple, you might like to ask a friend to go and stand about 29·5 km (or about 18 miles) further on holding a small cherry. That's Pluto. If you had lots of spare strange friends you could do the other planets too. This chart shows how far each planet is from the sun, its orbit time, what you need to model it and how far from the yellow tree everybody has to stand.

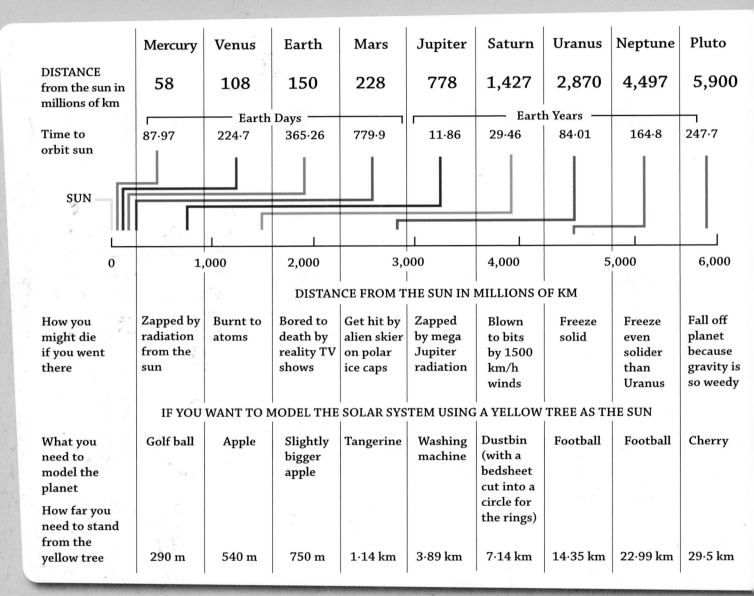

	Mercury	Venus	Earth	Mars	Jupiter	Saturn	Uranus	Neptune	Pluto
DISTANCE from the sun in millions of km	58	108	150	228	778	1,427	2,870	4,497	5,900
Time to orbit sun	87·97	224·7	365·26	779·9	11·86	29·46	84·01	164·8	247·7
How you might die if you went there	Zapped by radiation from the sun	Burnt to atoms	Bored to death by reality TV shows	Get hit by alien skier on polar ice caps	Zapped by mega Jupiter radiation	Blown to bits by 1500 km/h winds	Freeze solid	Freeze even solider than Uranus	Fall off planet because gravity is so weedy
What you need to model the planet	Golf ball	Apple	Slightly bigger apple	Tangerine	Washing machine	Dustbin (with a bedsheet cut into a circle for the rings)	Football	Football	Cherry
How far you need to stand from the yellow tree	290 m	540 m	750 m	1·14 km	3·89 km	7·14 km	14·35 km	22·99 km	29·5 km

(Time to orbit: Earth Days — Mercury, Venus, Earth, Mars; Earth Years — Jupiter, Saturn, Uranus, Neptune, Pluto)

SUN

DISTANCE FROM THE SUN IN MILLIONS OF KM
0   1,000   2,000   3,000   4,000   5,000   6,000

IF YOU WANT TO MODEL THE SOLAR SYSTEM USING A YELLOW TREE AS THE SUN

Recently, astronomers have found a few other tiny planety objects flying around the solar system. One of them is Sedna which is slightly smaller than Pluto. At the moment it's about twice as far away, but as it flies round the sun it moves up to 20 times further away than Pluto, and that's why it takes over 10,000 years just for one orbit! If you're wondering why we didn't find it years ago, it's like looking in the dark for a penny coin about 100 km (or 62 miles) away. Oh, there's one more thing. Sedna is so far away that sunlight hardly touches it, so that means your penny should be painted black.

WHY WE'RE ALL MOVING AT 18 MILES PER SECOND

As the Earth moves around the sun, sometimes it gets closer...

ARGHHH! WE'RE GOING TO GET COOKED BY THE SUN!

...and at other times it gets further away.

OH NO! WE'RE GOING TO DRIFT OFF INTO SPACE!

The reason for this is that planets move around the sun in ellipses, not circles. The sun is at one focus of the ellipse and there's nothing at the other one  43.

Earth's orbit around the sun is almost a perfect circle, so the distance doesn't change much.

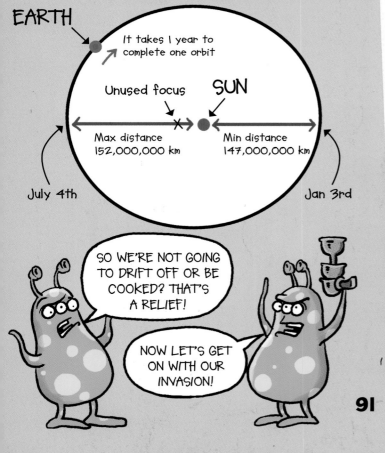

EARTH

It takes 1 year to complete one orbit

Unused focus

SUN

Max distance 152,000,000 km

Min distance 147,000,000 km

July 4th

Jan 3rd

SO WE'RE NOT GOING TO DRIFT OFF OR BE COOKED? THAT'S A RELIEF!

NOW LET'S GET ON WITH OUR INVASION!

HOW TO DRAW ELLIPSES

The old-fashioned way is to bang in two nails, put a loose loop of string around them and then draw round inside the loop with a pencil keeping the string tight. These days it's a lot easier to use a computer art program. But where's the fun in that, eh? Pass the hammer.

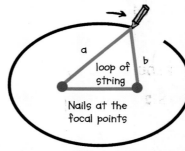

a

loop of string

b

Nails at the focal points

If you add length 'a' to length 'b' you always get the same answer. It doesn't matter where on the ellipse you've got your pencil.

A complete orbit of the sun is almost a billion kilometres long. As the Earth does one orbit every year, it needs to whizz along at about 30 km per second (or about 18 miles per second).

THAT'S TOO FAST FOR US! LET'S GET OUT OF HERE!

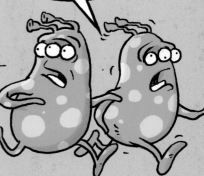

HOW PLANETS SPEED UP AND SLOW DOWN

Back in 1605, a German called Johannes Kepler discovered the most amazing law that describes how planets move faster when they are nearer to the sun.

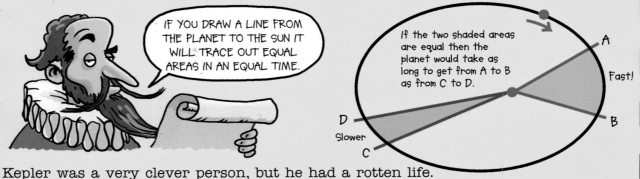

IF YOU DRAW A LINE FROM THE PLANET TO THE SUN IT WILL TRACE OUT EQUAL AREAS IN AN EQUAL TIME.

If the two shaded areas are equal then the planet would take as long to get from A to B as from C to D.

A

Fast!

B

D

Slower

C

Kepler was a very clever person, but he had a rotten life. At one point he had to save his wife from being burnt as a witch!

MONSTER STARS

If you thought the solar system was empty, the rest of space is even emptier! The nearest star to our own sun is Proxima Centauri which is 4·2 light years away.

If you're still standing 750 metres from a yellow tree holding an apple and grape, guess where you should paint the next yellow tree to represent Proxima Centauri? It's 200,000 km away – which is halfway to the moon!

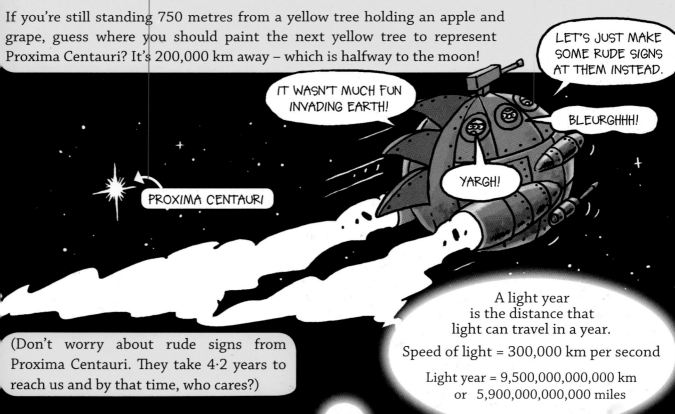

LET'S JUST MAKE SOME RUDE SIGNS AT THEM INSTEAD.

IT WASN'T MUCH FUN INVADING EARTH!

BLEURGHHH!

YARGH!

PROXIMA CENTAURI

(Don't worry about rude signs from Proxima Centauri. They take 4·2 years to reach us and by that time, who cares?)

A light year is the distance that light can travel in a year.

Speed of light = 300,000 km per second

Light year = 9,500,000,000,000 km
or 5,900,000,000,000 miles

Our sun is just a small yellow dwarf star but if you want to see two supergiants, look for the constellation of Orion. It has a very distinctive shape and can be seen in the night sky between December and March from anywhere on Earth.

The bright star at the south end is Rigel. It's a blue supergiant which is about 70 times wider than our sun and 40,000 times brighter. Although a few other stars look slightly brighter, that's because they are a lot closer to us than Rigel which is 773 light years away.

ORION THE HUNTER

BETELGEUSE

RIGEL

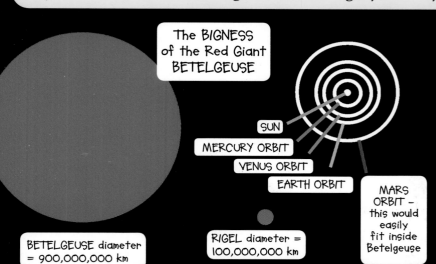

The BIGNESS of the Red Giant BETELGEUSE

SUN

MERCURY ORBIT

VENUS ORBIT

EARTH ORBIT

MARS ORBIT – this would easily fit inside Betelgeuse

BETELGEUSE diameter = 900,000,000 km

RIGEL diameter = 100,000,000 km

If you think Rigel's big, then Betelgeuse is a monster. It's the orangey-red star at the north end of Orion and it's a mere 427 light years away. It's about 650 times wider than our sun which makes it a lot bigger than the orbit of Mars.

HOW THE NUMBER 1 CONTROLS THE UNIVERSE

HOORAY, WE'RE OUT OF THE GALAXY!

WE'VE LEFT ALL THAT MURDEROUS MATHS BEHIND!

Actually there's no escaping Murderous Maths. Other subjects such as history or French or geography might not mean much in deep space, but 1 + 1 still equals 2 wherever you are. And as long as our little number 1 is behaving itself, it controls the universe. Remember how 1 started the Fibonacci series? And then that led to the equiangular spiral? ➡57

There are anything up to 400 billion stars in our galaxy – guess what shape they make? Yes, it's an equiangular spiral!

Fiendish facts

Since Lego was invented they have made about 400 billion bricks. If they were divided up evenly, everybody in the world would get 62 bricks each. A tower of 40 billion lego bricks would reach the moon. If you have six standard lego bricks (the ones with eight studs on top) there are about 915 million ways you can put them together.

There are ten times MORE stars in the night sky than grains of sand on all the world's beaches and deserts! A good telescope can see about 70 sextillion stars, which is a 7 followed by 22 zeros, but this is only a tiny number compared to the total number of stars in the universe!

STILL NOT HAD ENOUGH MURDEROUS MATHS? YOU'RE ALMOST AS FIENDISH AS ME! CHECK OUT MY FIENDISH FACTS...

One kiss can contain 40,000 parasites, 250 types of bacteria and up to 0.45 grams of FAT! So if you got kissed 2,222 times, your weight could go up by 1 kg.

...t has 30 billion working parts, its memory is about 4,000 gigabytes, it handles 86,000,000 bits of data every day via a data bus operating at 40hz. It processes 100,000 pixel images in focus at 25 frames/sec in 2,000,000 colours ... so wouldn't you like to have one? Well you do - it's your brain!

At any one time there are almost half a million people flying on aeroplanes.

The average person spend 2½ days every year on the toilet.

W.C.

80% of the zips in the world are made in one town! Every year the people of QIAOTOU, CHINA make enough zips to go right around the world FIVE times. (And just in case your trousers don't have a zip, you'll be interested to know that they also make 15 billion buttons a year, which is 60% of the world's total.)

A normal pencil measuring 18 cm can draw a line up to 55 km long (which is about 34 miles). It would be about 1.5 mm wide and the thickness on the paper will be about 4 millionths of a millimetre.

Time to go home

Goodbye, and thanks for joining us!
Obviously we haven't quite managed to fit absolutely every bit of maths about the whole of everything into one book, but rest assured, we have dealt with all the most important things.

Join the Murderous Maths gang for more fun, games and tips at www.murderousmaths.co.uk